50 Beautiful Deer-Resistant Plants

RUTH ROGERS CLAUSEN

50 Beautiful Deer-Resistant Plants

THE PRETTIEST ANNUALS, PERENNIALS, BULBS, AND SHRUBS THAT DEER DON'T EAT

Photographs by Alan L. Detrick

TIMBER PRESS
Portland * London

Published in 2011 by Timber Press, Inc.

The Haseltine Building
133 S.W. Second Avenue, Suite 450   6a Lonsdale Road
Portland, Oregon 97204-3527   London NW6 6RD
timberpress.com   timberpress.co.uk

Fifth printing 2015

Printed in China

Library of Congress Cataloging-in-Publication Data

Clausen, Ruth Rogers, 1938-
  50 beautiful deer-resistant plants : the prettiest annuals, perennials, bulbs,
and shrubs that deer don't eat / by Ruth Rogers Clausen ; photography by
Alan L. Detrick.
      p. cm.
  Includes bibliographical references and index.
  ISBN 978-1-60469-195-5
  1. Deer—Control—United States. 2. Plants, Ornamental—Disease and pest
resistance--United States. I. Detrick, Alan. II. Title. III. Title: Gardener's guide
to the best annuals, perennials, shrubs, ferns, bulbs, herbs, and grasses.
  SB994.D4C63 2011
  635.9'26965—dc22   2010051374

A catalog record for this book is also available from the British Library.

To all gardeners
who tend gardens
in deer country

Contents

Acknowledgments

I would like to thank all those who helped me along the way with this book and especially Tom Fischer at Timber Press, who suggested the project. Tom Christopher is always there for me with ideas and keeps me focused. Thank you to my husband, Don, who read and reread the text. Thank you to Margaret Barrett for her confidence and support. My thanks go to Alan and Linda Detrick, not only for Alan's beautiful photographs but also for their friendship and enthusiasm. Without Juree Sondker, Eve Goodman, and Mindy Fitch this project would not have been so complete.

Introduction

Considering the explosion of deer populations across the United States and the huge amount of damage that they inflict on rural, suburban, and even urban gardens and parks, it is no surprise that deer and gardeners are seldom compatible. But is it possible to achieve a beautiful, deer-resistant garden without resorting to fences, barriers, and toxic repellents? Indeed, you can still have a lush, thriving garden by making smart plant choices. Many stunning plants are unpalatable to deer because of their poisonous compounds, fuzzy or aromatic leaves, tough, spiny, or bristly textures, and for a variety of other less obvious reasons. This guide presents the most outstanding ornamental examples of these.

The "Bambi" syndrome is fine for those not plagued by deer. Of course deer are beautiful, and yes, they were sometimes (not always) here first, and they certainly deserve to live out their lives with full bellies as nature intended, but there is often not enough food for dense deer populations, and these animals are stressed by modern life and eradication of habitat. Since natural predators such as mountain lions and wolves have been largely eliminated, deer have been allowed to run out of control. A hundred years ago when year-round hunting was permitted, white-tailed deer numbers dropped, so hunters, fearing their sport would be ruined, urged laws to restrict hunting to about three to four months, from fall through Christmas. As the balance of nature was disrupted, white-tailed deer populations exploded.

Gardeners in different parts of the country are plagued by different species of deer. West of the Mississippi River, mule deer (*Odocoileus hemionus*) and black-tailed deer (*O. hemionus columbianus*) predominate. The latter is a subspecies of the former, smaller and stockier but just as hungry. In the East and

elsewhere, white-tailed deer (*O. virginianus*) make their home. Moose and elk are found in northern regions. While these species formerly lived on the edges of woods and forests, they have now discovered that there are easy and tasty sources of food in a new region called "the backyard."

Many books have dealt with this problem by suggesting unsightly fences. Few of us, though, would be happy to live within an enclosure unless the property was so large that you still felt free—small gardens should not make you feel like a zoo exhibit. Moreover, part of having a garden is surely an attitude of wanting to be part of nature rather than shutting yourself off. Sprays and repellents are fine if you are willing to keep up the work—not such an easy task in late spring and summer when tender new growth abounds, or in winter after each heavy rain or snowfall. Fortunately, there is another option: to focus on building a garden around the most beautiful and versatile deer-resistant plants.

This book presents the best plants to grow if you are striving for a pleasing garden but not prepared to spoil a long weekend away worrying whether deer will trash the garden in your absence. It is geared as a practical, user-friendly guide to successful gardening in deer country, based on observations made in countless gardens in the United States, Canada, and Europe, along with my own thirty-plus years of experience gardening in the Northeast.

The lion's share of this book is a directory of 50 exceptional deer-resistant plants, each categorized as an annual, perennial, shrub, fern, bulb, herb, or grass. In addition to describing the plant in question, I discuss how to grow it, provide design tips, and suggest deer-resistant companion plants, cultivars, and related species to try, all readily available in the marketplace.

Plant entries are arranged alphabetically by common name (for example, castor oil plant), with Latin or botanical names given secondarily (*Ricinus communis*). However, it is important to understand that common names may vary from region to region, while Latin names remain the same worldwide. It is worth getting comfortable with the botanical names of plants

(previous page top) A deer helps himself to tomatoes in a backyard.

(bottom) This border is planted with seldom-browsed purple catmint, yellow yarrow, mauve hardy geranium, and deep purple hybrid sage.

so that you actually get the plant you were seeking rather than another with the same common name.

Plant hardiness zones provided in each entry refer to the United States Department of Agriculture map that can be found in many mail-order catalogs or on the USDA website: usna.usda.gov/Hardzone/ushzmap.html. These zone numbers are based on average annual minimum winter temperatures:

Below –50°F	Zone 1	Below –46°C
–50° to –40°F	Zone 2	–46° to –40°C
–40° to –30°F	Zone 3	–40° to –34°C
–30° to –20°F	Zone 4	–34° to –29°C
–20° to –10°F	Zone 5	–29° to –23°C
–10° to 0°F	Zone 6	–23° to –18°C
0° to 10°F	Zone 7	–18° to –12°C
10° to 20°F	Zone 8	–12° to –7°C
20° to 30°F	Zone 9	–7° to –1°C
30° to 40°F	Zone 10	–1° to 4°C
above 40°	Zone 11	above 4°C

Selecting plants according to your zone will maximize their potential, but these zones serve only as a guide—adventurous gardeners will want to "push the zones" of favorite plants. Remember, however, that tough, strong plants are less likely to be destroyed by deer than struggling, weak ones. They must do more than just survive. Learn from nurseries, neighbors, and public gardens what plants do well in your climate, and contact Cooperative Extension offices for lists of deer-resistant plants by state. Some plants may not tolerate heat and high humidity well. Lamb's ears (*Stachys byzantina*), for instance, thrive in dry Southern California but "melt" in the same zone number in Florida and the Gulf Coast. Summer hardiness is also an issue. The USDA has a summer hardiness map based on the premise that some plants will not tolerate excessive, unrelieved heat, but this map is not widely used by residential gardeners. Winter hardiness is greatly affected by soil drainage. Many plants, especially those from high-altitude and Mediterranean regions, are accustomed to very free draining (well-drained) soil. Winter wet is the bane of these, and gardeners with heavy clay soils are reminded to amend their soil thoroughly before planting. Many plants die from wet feet.

The deer resistance rating given at the top of each entry ranks the plant's resistance to deer on a scale of 1 to 10. Each plant is rated within a range. A rating of 7 indicates that deer sometimes nip off flowers but leave the foliage alone, as with signet marigold (*Tagetes tenuifolia*); 8 indicates that just one or two flowers may be nibbled or destroyed, but the plant is otherwise left alone, as with peony (*Paeonia officinalis*); 9 indicates that deer occasionally browse young spring foliage but mostly ignore the plant, as with purple beautyberry (*Callicarpa dichotoma*); and 10 indicates that deer very seldom browse foliage or flowers and usually avoid the plant altogether, as with rosemary (*Rosmarinus officinalis*). Plants that deer regularly feed on and that would be listed as lower than 7 are not included in this book. Hydrangeas, for example, would be rated 3 to 6, mountain laurels 3 to 5, and deer candy such as hostas, lilies, and daylilies 1 to 3.

It is important to note that although plants rated at 10 are rarely browsed by deer, there is no such thing as a deer-proof plant. During times of extreme hunger stress, deer will eat anything to survive, including plants that are usually ignored because they are unpalatable, or even those deemed poisonous to deer. Herds also differ in their preferences; even herds living just a few miles apart may have very different tastes. In addition, deer may devour a particular plant one year and ignore it the next, so it is wise to avoid letting down your guard. The deer resistance ratings in this book are based on the reports, research, and experience of others across the United States and my own experience in the Northeast where white-tailed deer abound. Since no plants are unconditionally, always, ig-

Deer resistance ratings
Each plant is rated on a scale from 7 to 10. Note that plants rated lower than 7, those regularly browsed by deer, are not included in this book.

7 — Deer sometimes nip off flowers but leave foliage alone

8 — Deer occasionally nip off one or two flowers but mostly ignore plant

9 — Deer occasionally browse young spring foliage but mostly ignore plant

10 — Deer rarely browse foliage or flowers and usually avoid plant altogether

nored by deer, these ratings must only be considered a guide. No doubt some readers whose local herds behave differently will take issue with the deer-resistance numbers for particular plants.

If the nucleus of your garden is composed of the plants examined in this book, you will be able to have your garden and enjoy it too. These are the best, most stunning and versatile plants to help solve one of the most ubiquitous problems in gardening. Rather than constructing fences and barriers, you can deter deer with your smart, beautiful plant choices.

Help!
Deer Are Destroying My Garden

THIS CHAPTER is aimed at helping you understand and work around deer behavior, and to give you a sense of the variety of methods gardeners use to attempt to deter these animals. Deer need safe places to sleep, rest, and eat. They are creatures of habit, and knowing some of their habits makes it easier to design garden spaces they will avoid. By denying the herd cover, water, and food, you can make them feel uncomfortable enough that they will want to move elsewhere. And working to prevent deer from nibbling your garden is better than trying to keep them under control once they are already enjoying it.

If you aspire to have a deer-tolerant garden, the tips provided here will come in handy. In the end, however, we gardeners must decide whether we want to remain bound to gardens that need constant protection from deer, inevitably frustrating ourselves in the endeavor, or whether we can change our habit of planting deer favorites like hostas, daylilies, roses, lilies, and tulips. So many beautiful deer-resistant garden plants are available, why not use them? The more we learn about these alternatives, the more relaxed and successful we will be in our gardens.

Signs of Deer Traffic

Several telltale signs will let you know that deer have visited, even before your hostas have been eaten to a nub. Ideally you

In the Brine Garden, New York, a quiet path is lined with billowy native switch grass (*Panicum*) and *Ligularia* species.

will then be able to take precautions before more serious damage occurs.

In late summer and fall, you may see freshly raw places on the stems or trunks of young trees and shrubs where the bark has been skinned. These are called buck rubs. This occurs when bucks find a handy, usually deciduous, tree or shrub on which to remove the velvet from their antlers. Later on, the bucks again damage saplings as they mark territory prior to the rutting season. The open wounds on the branch or trunk can cause the plant to dry out or even die.

Deer scat is often evident on lawns or in the woods. The droppings are larger than those of rabbits, and clustered in a group. In mud and wet places beside streams and ponds, footprints may also be evident. Deer are cloven-hoofed mammals

(as are cows and sheep), so the print appears as if there are two toes.

Most important to gardeners, of course, is finding browsed twigs, foliage, and flowers. Deer have no upper incisor teeth and must tear off their food, so ragged, torn vegetation is a sure sign they have been feeding. Check twigs on azaleas and rhododendrons, young hosta and daylily leaves, decapitated tulips, and the like. Deer cannot nip off twigs cleanly as rabbits and woodchucks do. In shrub borders, woods, or along highways you may notice that plants are almost naked from about 5 ft. down to ground level. They have been eaten to a particular height, resulting in the plants having a "topknot" of foliage but nothing much at the base. If you can afford to, buy more mature trees with trunks that have already grown above the browsing height of deer. (Imagine if you had to deal with browsing giraffes!)

(left) Bucks use tree trunks to rid their antlers of velvet, leaving the trunks scarred.

(right) Deer footprints.

This fence was erected too late to save these evergreens. Deer have eaten the lower branches, sparing only the out-of- reach topknots of vegetation. New growth, however, has developed lower on the trunks since the fence was installed.

Times to Expect High Deer Pressure

Pressure from deer fluctuates according to time of year and type of season. Deer usually feed at dusk and dawn, although it often appears that your garden has been eaten all night long. They prefer to feed close to cover, but if hungry enough will go out into open areas.

Winter is the worst time for deer, especially in cold parts of the northern United States and Canada. With little food available they will eat almost anything they can reach, including bird seed from feeders, prized dwarf evergreens, and developing buds of deciduous trees and shrubs. Many will die of starvation rather than the cold. Warm slopes (south-facing in the northern hemisphere) are favorite gathering places for deer herds during cold weather, especially if a food source like bird feeders can be found nearby. Their metabolism slows down in winter, so they can get by with less food, but they lose heat easily and huddle together for warmth. Once they find your garden in winter, they will return each year throughout their lives, so it is important to deter them from the outset.

As spring comes, the does give birth and have high nutrition needs. The fawns learn quickly from their mothers and if born on your property will always return to feed there. The mothers teach the fawns which plants are good to eat and which to avoid. Not much food is around, as it has been eaten during the winter, but deer are hungrier and will travel further afield to find it. Where they may not have invaded your yard previously, it will become a regular stopping place once discovered. Later there will be plenty of food around, but new spring plantings still need protection. Deer are very curious. Even if they are not hungry, they often take a bite of a newly planted seedling or transplant, plucking it out of the ground, spitting it out, and leaving it to dry out and die.

Through the summer when food is plentiful, deer don't need to feed from your garden, but habits are hard to break. If you have prepared a landscape buffet, they will undoubtedly come, since the food will be much more palatable and easier to get than in the wild. During dry times in summer, deer are not only hungry but also thirsty. Garden plants that have just been watered or sprinkled are perfect for them, especially if the leaves remain wet at dusk.

High-protein acorns, beechnuts, and dropped orchard fruits and crab apples, along with poison ivy berries, make up a large part of their diet in fall when they are preparing for the rut or mating season. Garden damage is not confined to food during this time: buck rubs on young trees and shrubs cause great damage, and signposting, a way of imprinting their scent on woody plants and on the ground to deter other bucks, is also a nuisance.

This perennial has been eaten by deer. Note the ragged tears on the leaves.

This sign reminds visitors to close the gate.

Commonly Used Controls

Passionate gardeners living in deer country will try anything to keep their gardens free from deer damage. Controls range from inexpensive home remedies to top-of-the-line deer fences and electronic products, all promising to be the perfect remedy.

Physical barriers

A physical barrier is the only reliable way of keeping deer out of a yard, but even that is not foolproof if the gate is left open. Before installing any type of fencing, check your local building codes. Experts in wildlife management recommend a fence 8 ft. high made of woven wire. Even during times when deer pressure is high, these fences do their job, and they can be erected to protect a large area or a single specimen tree or shrub. However, they are also expensive to install and not very attractive. And where bedrock is close to the surface or the terrain is steep, they may not even be practical. Are they there to keep the deer out or the homeowners in?

Heavy-duty plastic mesh is a less expensive fencing product that is attached to trees or posts around the property. Typically it is black and hardly visible from a distance. It must be fastened securely at ground level to prevent deer from slipping underneath. Double fences often work well and don't need to be as high. Two parallel 4-ft. high fences installed about 3 to 4 ft. apart are sufficient as deer are cautious about getting caught between them. Electric fencing must be installed professionally, and some areas have local ordinances in respect to electric fences on residential property, so check those out first. The wires or aluminum flags may be smeared with peanut butter to attract deer and give them a good deterring jolt when they lick it. Heavy-duty fishing line is inexpensive and reportedly effective in some gardens. Lines of monofilament are strung from trees or posts at 1-ft. intervals from 6 in. above ground level. Whatever type of fence is erected, it is important to attach flags or ribbons right away; this is to alert the deer so they don't go flying into the barrier, destroying it and themselves in the process. Brad Roeller, an expert on deer behavior for-

merly at the Cary Institute of Ecosystem Studies, New York, recommends that you complete any installation as quickly as possible, ideally within twenty-four hours, so that deer don't have time to find any penetrable holes.

(left) Deer cannot get to this star magnolia.

(right) Flags warn deer of a new fence.

Smaller-scale protection

In cold winter areas where shrubs are vulnerable to deer browsing, many gardeners put black plastic or nylon netting over their shrubs to protect them. Inexpensive, lightweight, 1-in. mesh plastic or nylon netting can be bought in rolls or smaller packages from garden centers nationwide. The material is draped over the particular plant or hedge and secured to posts so that deer cannot get underneath. It can be used for several years and after removal in spring is often used to protect beds of tulips or daylilies.

Buck rubs are disfiguring at best and lethal to young trees and shrubs at worst. They usually occur on thin-barked spe-

Lightweight netting protects tulips just before their peak.

cies. Wrap the trunks and low major branches of the trees and shrubs with burlap or other material. Several commercial products are on the market for this purpose, including spiral vinyl tree wraps (orchardvalleysupply.com) and poly roll tree wrap (frostproof.com). Snow fencing erected around the stems or trunk is another option.

Scare tactics may help as well. Barking dogs mostly do a good job of keeping deer at bay. Take them walking along the perimeter of the yard, encouraging them to pee at frequent intervals. Deer have an excellent sense of smell and will be deterred from entering the property. Motion-activated water sprinklers (aimergard.com) and electronic deer repellents are on the market, too, with spotty beneficial results. In some gardens they seem to work well, but elsewhere the deer just stand and look at them. They are marketed under such names as DeerChaser electronic deer repellent and 18-in. Havahart electronic deer repellent spikes.

Loud noises may disturb neighbors and cause friction, but wind chimes are usually pleasant-sounding to people while simultaneously deterring deer. Several chimes at different pitches in the yard can be effective.

Repellents and home remedies

The market abounds with commercial deer repellents, mostly based on bad or bitter taste (Deer Off, Deer Away) or pungent smell (Garlic Barrier, Hinder, Plantskydd). Some work better in one garden than in another, and they are most effective if you change your product from month to month. Apply several different products throughout the season, as deer pressure increases or decreases. If there has been little damage and no deer sightings for a while, don't be lulled into a false sense of security, as deer will surely return. Commercial repellents may be liquid or granular. Granular products such as Deer Scram and Milorganite are easier to apply but may not last as long

(left) The burlap trunk wrapping on this young elm prevents bucks from rubbing against the stem.

(right) Wind chimes make a pleasing sound and may help to deter deer.

A bar of smelly soap hung to deter deer.

during damp weather. Liquid remedies such as Liquid Fence always contain a sticking agent so that they adhere better to foliage, but new applications must be made after heavy rain and as the plants grow. Some are temperature sensitive and should only be used if the temperature is above freezing. Use granular products in cold weather rather than spraying liquids that could cause damage. Dried blood and several other products are fertilizers as well as repellents and should just be sprinkled around beds as recommended. Fish emulsion, such as Coast of Maine fermented salmon, is an excellent fertilizer that also happens to offend deer noses. Be careful not to overfertilize, however, which will result in the soft, succulent vegetative growth that deer love. Just half the recommended dosage at a given time will leave the odor but not overstimulate the plants. Some experts suggest soaking pieces of rag or cotton balls in predator urine (wolf, coyote, lion) or other repellents, putting them in discarded hosiery, and hanging them around your property. Try to camouflage them in the bushes, as they are not pretty. Human hair may also be used as a deterrent. Collect hair from your local barber (or cat and dog hair from pet parlors) and strew it around the garden or hang it in sachets from tree limbs. It will decompose in time. Bars of strong-smelling soap hung from trees and shrubs sometimes work but don't last long in wet climates.

If you intend to use repellents, it is important to apply them regularly and routinely, especially after heavy rain or snow. Repellents are not useful after the plants have been eaten, although they may deter a return devastation. Always read the instructions on repellents carefully.

Feeding stations

It might seem as though a feeding station at the edge of the property stocked with alfalfa or corn would keep deer occupied at that location, away from your prize dahlias, but deer seldom remain in a single spot and soon discover the rest of the garden. It's also illegal to feed wildlife in some states, and it's not worth risking a summons.

Designing a Deer-Resistant Garden

Some gardeners seem to shy away from the term "deer-resistant plants," almost as if such plants must be the runts of the litter. Nothing could be further from the truth. Deer favorites such as roses, daylilies, and tulips are not the only showy, attractive garden plants around. You can create a spectacular garden using the plants described in this book. Deer-resistant plants lend themselves to many garden styles, but especially to mixed beds and borders, wildlife gardens, and native plant and wildflower gardens.

Where to grow

Mixed beds and borders include small trees and shrubs with perennials, bulbs, annuals, and often groundcovers. They can be formal or informal, simple or complicated, depending upon the setting and the way you handle them, but in deer country, plants that deer avoid should constitute the main plant palate.

Play with some combinations that please you, always coming back to plants that you are reasonably confident will not attract deer. Try a backdrop of shrubs such as spring-blooming pink weigela, Japanese spirea (*Spiraea japonica*), bush cinque-

This little bed planted with box-wood and surrounded with grape hyacinths for spring will not be destroyed by deer.

foil (*Potentilla fruticosa*), and boxwoods. Tough, spiny rugosa rose (*Rosa rugosa*), one of the few roses that deer don't damage, makes a nice backdrop, too. In front, plant drifts of bulbs for spring, including early-blooming snowdrops (*Galanthus*), white-eyed blue or pink glory-of-the-snow (*Chionodoxa*), Siberian squills (*Scilla sibirica*), and daffodils located close to the shrubs since the foliage takes a few weeks to ripen. (Notice that tulips are not on this list.) Add perennials and shrubs of different heights to carry the border through to summer and on to fall. For sunny gardens consider hardy geraniums (*Geranium*), hummingbird mints (*Agastache*), globe thistle (*Echinops*), *Artemisia* 'Silver Mound' for foliage contrast, different sages (*Salvia*), catmint (*Nepeta*), and tickseed (*Coreopsis*). Seldom are any of these damaged by deer, and they constitute a splendid array of colors, forms, and heights to grace any border. Perhaps add a tidy edging of lamb's ears (*Stachys byzantina*), as favored by one celebrated East Coast garden writer. In shade the palate is no less varied, even without hostas, rhododendrons, and azaleas. For shrubs, try a selection of deer-resistant spicebush (*Lindera*), Japanese plum yew (*Cephalotaxus*), late-blooming summersweet (*Clethra*), and Oregon holly grape (*Mahonia*). Most spring-flowering bulbs do fine in light shade, especially under deciduous trees, as bloom is over by the time the trees leaf out. With them try Siberian bugloss (*Brunnera*), wild ginger (*Asarum*), and hellebores (*Helleborus*) that bloom during the daffodil season. Ferns begin to emerge then and remain good-looking all season. If the soil is damp, tall graceful cinnamon fern is wonderful, while in drier places lower-growing Japanese painted fern and autumn fern are showy. Mix in some low evergreens toward the foreground for a change in texture; fragrant sweet box (*Sarcococca*) and Japanese skimmia (*Skimmia*) are prime candidates. Fringed bleeding heart (*Dicentra eximia*), coral bells (*Heuchera*), and foamflower (*Tiarella*) in various leaf colors and patterns, and white and pastel-colored astilbes could furnish the front and midground. For spring, forget-me-nots (*Myosotis*) and bigroot geranium (*Geranium macrorrhizum*) make a colorful show. Stately black snakeroot (*Actaea racemosa*) with its tall, white bottlebrush flowers and yellow-spiked rocket ligularia (*Ligularia* 'The Rocket') keep the interest going. Plant patches of autumn crocus (*Colchicum*) throughout. You won't miss hostas at all.

Wildlife gardens are those planted with species to attract wildlife of all kinds (including deer) but especially hummingbirds and other birds, butterflies, bees, and insects. Berry- and seed-bearing trees and shrubs such as winterberry (*Ilex verticillata*), spicebush (*Lindera benzoin*), shadbush (*Amelanchier*), and cornelian cherry (*Cornus mas*) often make up a large proportion of the space, providing cover and resting places as well as food. Plenty of deer-resistant perennials provide nectar and resting places, too. Plant hummingbird mints (*Agastache*), ornamental oregano (*Origanum*), dame's rocket (*Hesperis*), beebalm (*Monarda*), and so many others in the mint family. Don't forget to add larval food plants, which are essential if you want to

'Moonbeam' threadleaf coreopsis
(*Coreopsis verticillata* 'Moonbeam').

enjoy butterflies later. Butterfly weed (*Asclepias tuberosa*) and other milkweeds, for example, provide food for Monarch caterpillars. For detailed information, refer to Jeffrey Glassberg's *Butterflies of North America* or the North American Butterfly Association website (naba.org).

A wildflower garden is for so-called wildflowers. These may be native or exotic but naturalize freely. Deer-resistant Queen Anne's lace (*Daucus carota*), butter and eggs (*Linaria vulgaris*), lesser celandine (*Ranunculus ficaria*), and wild fennel (*Foeniculum vulgare*), for instance, are considered wildflowers, though all hail from other parts of the world. They have adapted to new conditions and made themselves too much at home in the United States and Canada, so try to select natives where possible.

Native plant gardens are planted exclusively with true native plants, which vary from region to region. Deer depend upon lots of native plants for their diet, but they also tend to avoid many natives, and these we must seek out. Some native plant enthusiasts have a very strict definition of native plants, while others interpret it more loosely, for example including Louisiana natives growing in a midwestern garden, California species growing in Pennsylvania, or Delaware natives growing in Ontario. A native plant garden does not have to be messy and unkempt, as some suggest. Beautiful gardens planted with deer-resistant natives can be as sophisticated and lovely as any. A fine example designed by Stephanie Cohen can be found on the campus of Temple University, Pennsylvania. Another often unresolved point of contention refers to cultivars or selections of natives. For example, does 'Moonbeam', a cultivar of native threadleaf coreopsis, *Coreopsis verticillata*, have a place in a native plant garden? Other deer-unfriendly natives, some with plenty of cultivars, include coral bells (*Heuchera*), beebalm (*Monarda*), tickseeds (*Coreopsis*), quamash (*Camassia*), many ferns, Allegheny spurge (*Pachysandra procumbens*), switch grass (*Panicum*) and some other ornamental grasses, hummingbird mints (*Agastache*), and sages (*Salvia*).

Characteristics of plants that deer avoid

Although no plant is completely deer-proof, certain generalizations can be made about plants that deer are likely to ignore. Fuzzy-leaved plants seem to be unpalatable to deer—the hairs on the leaves must be irritating to the tongue. Lamb's ears (*Stachys byzantina*), licorice plant (*Helichrysum petiolare*), and lady's mantle (*Alchemilla mollis*) are good examples. Some plants contain compounds that are poisonous to mammals and deer in particular. By instinct or because they were taught by their mothers, deer detect the presence of these compounds, though in desperate hunger situations they will resort to eating them. Spurges (*Euphorbia*) and Lenten roses (*Helleborus orientalis*) are among these, along with castor oil plant (*Ricinus communis*) and monkshoods (*Aconitum*). Deer have an excellent sense of smell and get confused when overstimulated by aromatic or fragrant

(left) This striped lily-of-the-valley is as fragrant as it is beautiful.

(right) Siberian iris (*Iris sibirica* 'Silver Edge') rarely shows damage from deer.

foliage or flowers. Many culinary herbs fall into this category, such as sages (*Salvia*), rosemary (*Rosmarinus officinalis*), thymes (*Thymus*), and ornamental onions (*Allium*). Highly scented flowers like lilacs (*Syringa*), sweet alyssum (*Lobularia maritima*), and lily-of-the-valley (*Convallaria*) are seldom browsed. Plant these at entry points in the garden to confuse deer. Deer also dislike tough, leathery, or fibrous-textured foliage. Ferns and ornamental grasses belong here along with Japanese pachysandra (*Pachysandra terminalis*), peony (*Paeonia officinalis*), and Siberian iris (*Iris sibirica*). Spiny or bristly plants are also left alone. Spiky yucca (*Yucca filamentosa*), bristly poppies, rugosa roses (*Rosa rugosa* and its hybrids), globe thistle (*Echinops ritro*), and barberry (*Berberis*) are usually safe. In fact, due to lack of browsing by deer, pesky Japanese barberry (*Berberis thunbergii*) has spread through woodlands across North America, driving out native species for habitat. It is now included on many state lists of invasive species.

Plant barriers

Make it as difficult as possible for deer to use your garden as a buffet and playground. Look for tracks and deer paths so that you know just where deer are entering your garden, and head them off. In lieu of a fence, plant a dense shrubbery of tall, unpalatable plants that blocks their view of your garden beyond. 'Lynwood' forsythia (*Forsythia ×intermedia* 'Lynwood'), fragrant sumac (*Rhus racemosa*), arrowwood viburnum (*Viburnum dentatum*), tall cultivars of bush cinquefoil (*Potentilla fruticosa* 'Coronation Triumph', 'Jackmanii'), devil's walking stick (*Aralia spinosa*), dwarf Alberta spruce (*Picea glauca* 'Conica'), and trifoliate orange (*Poncirus trifoliata*) are good candidates. Or install and plant a tall trellis where they enter your garden. Deer are uncomfortable jumping into a space if they can't see a safe landing point. Trumpet vine (*Campsis radicans*), trumpet honeysuckle (*Lonicera sempervirens*), and Dutchman's pipe (*Aristolochia macrophylla*) are deer-resistant vines suitable to camouflage or decorate a tall trellis.

Change the terrain

Create berms or different ground levels at the entry points to wrong-foot deer. If you plant on top of berms you will gain extra height to hide your garden beyond. Construct terraces and steps on steep or sloping areas within the garden. Deer are uncomfortable navigating changing levels, especially when they are on the run. While they will readily walk up or down sloping ground, they are afraid to jump from level to level.

Cultural techniques

Deer like their food fresh and lush as well as easy to find. Soft, young daylily shoots, for example, are more palatable than older, fibrous stems. Grow your plants lean and cut down

Make terraces, landings, and steps on steep slopes.

33

on fertilizing. High-nitrogen fertilizers (those with a high first number on the label formula) encourage soft, disease- and deer-prone foliage. It is thought that deer actually need a diet high in nitrogen for good health. If well prepared and amended ahead of planting, few soils (except those for high-density succession vegetable gardens) need to be fertilized every year. Spot feed those few plants that are hungry feeders, such as peonies and astilbes.

Maintain soil fertility with regular applications of organic matter such as compost, decomposed leaves, or well-rotted manure, all of which improve the tilth, structure of the soil, and drainage without encouraging soft, deer-favored growth. Plants are able to reach their potential with good soil conditions, rooting deeply to tap into water and nutrients. If you fertilize with chemicals, select a slow-release, balanced formula such as 5-5-5 that does not shock the plants into quick soft growth. Look for the plant food formula on the package. The first number represents available nitrogen (N) for vegetative growth; the second number represents available phosphorus (P) for root, seed, and flower development; the third number represents available potassium (K) for flower and fruit development and increases sturdiness against stress and the elements. Save high-nitrogen fertilizer for leafy crops such as lettuce and salad greens.

Water wisely, especially during times of drought. Rather than sprinkling just a little every day, water deeply once a week or so to encourage deep rooting and strong, sturdy, less palatable plants. During dry spells especially, leaves that are wet in the evening are sure targets for nighttime deer browsing. If you are watering by hand or with a sprinkler, do it early in the morning or in early evening so the foliage dries off before nightfall. Better yet, use economical soaker hoses or drip irrigation to water at ground level and avoid soaking the leaves. If leaves remain wet going into the night, they are also more susceptible to the development of fungal diseases. Expect to find greater deer pressure in your garden during summer droughts.

Irrigate at ground level with a soaker hose to avoid wetting the foliage.

Deer candy

This list of plants that deer find appetizing is far from complete but identifies some definite plants to avoid.

* Annual phlox
* Azalea
* Blueberry
* Calibrachoa
* Chrysanthemum
* Clematis
* Coleus
* Corn
* Cosmos
* Crab apple
* Daylily

* Hydrangea
* Impatiens
* Lettuce and leafy crops
* Lily
* Magnolia
* Mountain laurel
* Nemesia
* Orchard fruits
* Osteospermum
* Pansy
* Petunia
* Pumpkin
* Rhododendron
* Rose (not rugosa rose)
* Scarlet runner bean
* Solomon's seal

* Strawberry
* Summer phlox
* Sunflower
* Sweet pea
* Sweet potato vine
* Torenia
* Tulip
* Viola
* White pine
* Yew
* Zonal geranium (not hardy geranium)

(top) Hostas, the ultimate deer candy, are interplanted with un-palatable ferns in light shade.

(next page) Tulips, wallflowers, violas, and mountain bluets (*Centaurea montana* 'Amethyst Dream') are less likely to be browsed by deer when planted in containers close to the house.

Keep lawn grass short, not only because it removes a hiding and feeding place but also because of the danger of deer ticks, which cause Lyme disease. Children and pets playing on lawns often pick up deer ticks. If the soil has been prepared properly prior to seeding or sodding, the roots should be able to reach down to the water table and not need daily sprinkling. A deep watering once or twice a week during dry spells should suffice. Forget extra fertilizer. It only encourages lush, soft leaves that grow more quickly and need more frequent mowing.

Avoid planting deer candy—a species known to attract deer—unless you are prepared to adequately protect it. Most of us can live without daylilies and tulips if we can have the joy of yarrows and daffodils. If not, you'll need to protect your favorite susceptible plants. Deer candy can be surrounded with deer-resistant plants; for example, in sun, aromatic savory calamint (*Calamintha nepeta*), lavender, bluebeard (*Caryopteris*),

or Russian sage (*Perovskia*) can be planted among and around roses and lilies to protect them.

Include water-thrifty plants, which also often resist browsing. These tend to have coarse cell walls that are difficult for deer to digest, making them less palatable. A sampling includes yarrows (*Achillea*), blue false indigo (*Baptisia australis*), blanket flower (*Gaillardia*), catmint (*Nepeta*), hummingbird mints (*Agastache*), Thunberg bush clover (*Lespedeza thunbergii*), lavenders (*Lavandula*), and many plants from Mediterranean and dry regions. Their structure evolved to help them survive periods of low water supply. Drought-tolerant plants may be planted anywhere in the garden but are especially useful in xeric gardens, planted often, but not only, in the Southwest. As water becomes a scarcer and more expensive commodity, responsible gardeners are becoming more careful about their watering habits. They are seeking and enjoying more plants that demand less water to thrive. Part of the garden that is not serviced by a water standpipe is by necessity a low-water garden.

Limb up low overhanging branches of crab apples, magnolias, orchard fruits, and other susceptible species to a height of at least 6 ft. This eliminates the line of vegetation that deer can browse. Keep underbrush to a minimum to remove a food source and hiding place. This is especially important on the edge of woodlands where deer like to hide and rest unobserved. Soft bedding of leaves, pine needles, ferns, or other vegetation is an open invitation for them to hang around.

Extra tips

Plants grown in containers close to the house on porches, decks, and terraces are less likely to be browsed, though of course there is no guarantee—it is not unusual to find one or more deer right at the back door in the morning. Try using hanging baskets, making sure they are high enough so that deer cannot reach them, no matter how close they are to the house.

(next page top) White-flowered redbud (*Cercis canadensis* 'Alba') limbed up above the browse line to prevent deer damage.

(next page bottom left) These hanging baskets are higher than deer can reach.

(next page bottom right) High, out-of-reach bird feeders near the house are less likely to attract deer.

Elevate bird feeders beyond the reach of deer, to at least 6 ft, and remove any brush or debris that could give deer a leg up. In snowy winters you may find deer climbing up on snow banks for an evening meal from your feeders. If possible, set bird feeders away from woodland edges where deer are likely to venture. Select feeders that can be raised or lowered on pulleys, enabling you to fill them easily yet still keep the food out of reach. Bird feeders positioned close to the house are a joy to those inside.

Decorations for the garden come in all sizes, shapes, and types, and some can scare deer quite effectively. Ornaments that catch light, such as shiny gazing balls, work in some gardens. If it fits your style, install a decoration with moving parts to frighten deer and discourage them from stopping. Though hardly ornamental, aluminum pie plates are sometimes effective when hung from trees or made into mobiles, particularly in vegetable gardens. Homemade flapping scarecrows can be fun and effective, too.

Mast (acorns) is a basic deer food, so be diligent about raking up acorns in the fall if oak trees grow on or near your property. Expect to experience greater deer pressure in years when acorns are in short supply. Pick up crab apples and orchard fruits routinely too, as these constitute a deer feast. Grapes, peaches, cherries, plums, and nectarine are other favorites.

Acorns and other deer-attracting foods must be picked up regularly.

(previous page) This glistening blue ginger jar catches the light and may spook deer.

Annuals

Most deer will ignore this simple annual border edged with boxwood. Floss flower (*Ageratum houstonianum* 'Blue Horizon'), flowering tobacco (*Nicotiana* 'Lime Green'), and blood sage (*Salvia coccinea* 'Snow Nymph') make a restful combination.

Castor oil plant

Ricinus communis

CASTOR OIL PLANT has become widespread in tropical areas of the world but is native to India and tropical Africa. Its seeds were found in Egyptian tombs. Perennial in frost-free areas, the plant may reach treesize proportions; in colder regions it seldom tops 12 ft. These outsized plants are sometimes massed as temporary screens but are more often used as focal points or in-ground "dot" plants or "thrillers" in containers. Cannas are frequent companions, but where deer pressure is heavy, sword-leaved New Zealand flax (*Phormium tenax*) or 'Burgundy Giant' fountain grass (*Pennisetum* 'Burgundy Giant') might be substituted to provide contrasting form, color, and texture.

Today castor oil is used in the making of biodiesel alternative fuels, but earlier generations will remember it as a dreaded medical remedy. In the garden this exotic-looking plant's architectural form, colorful prickly seedpods, and bold-fingered leaves embody the tropical look so popular with Victorians and now fashionable once more. Be aware that castor oil plant is the source of deadly ricin, which is why deer leave it alone. It should not be grown near playgrounds or where children could ingest parts of the plant, especially the beautifully marked seeds ("beans")—it is reported that just one can kill a child.

HOW TO GROW

Plants of castor oil plant are hard to find in local nurseries due to the danger of them being eaten, but seeds are available from mail-order seed houses. Start seeds indoors at about 75°F in individual pots. Wait until day temperatures are reliably 60°F to put out young plants. Always wear disposable gloves when handling the seeds.

QUICK LOOK

Hardiness
Annual

Height and spread
5–12 ft. × 2–4 ft.

Deer resistance rating
9–10

Castor oil plant in fruit (*Ricinus communis*).

This exotic-looking plant's architectural form, colorful prickly seedpods, and bold-fingered leaves embody the tropical look so popular with Victorians and now fashionable once more.

DESIGN TIPS

In residential gardens, castor oil plants are suitable where there is room for them to show off. If space is limited, plant them in large containers on a deck or patio to create a tropical ambience. Dwarf cultivars such as 4-ft. tall 'Impala', with red-flushed foliage and stems, are best in windy spots. Bronze-leaved, scarlet-fruited 'Carmencita' is widely grown in large planters and in the ground. At 6 to 8 ft. tall it makes a fine privacy screen for the summer when planted close, perhaps along a fence. For drama add 5- to 7-ft. tall, bright orange Mexican sunflower (*Tithonia rotundifolia* 'Torch') or 4-ft. tall, white or pink spider flower (*Cleome hassleriana* 'White Queen') in front. If you need more height, plant 'Zanzibarensis' (may reach 10 ft. or more) behind. Its massive, star-shaped leaves are dark green with white veins. Bronze-leaved 'Carmencita Pink' has pink flowers and seed capsules.

In-ground plantings of castor oil plant need not be confined to formal, Victorian, parklike designs. These imposing plants are perfect for the back of the border, especially when partnered with other tropicals such as copper leaf (*Acalypha wilkesiana*), Mexican shrubby spurge (*Euphorbia cotinifolia*), and upright shrub verbena (*Lantana camara*). Cassava or manihot (*Manihot esculenta*) is another valuable companion, especially 'Variegata'. Although dahlias look wonderful alongside castor oil plant, deer enjoy them too much.

Dusty miller

Senecio cineraria

SENECIO CINERARIA, *S. viravira, Artemisia stelleriana,* and *Tanacetum ptarmiciflorum* are all commonly known as dusty miller, a reference to the silvery gray or white, mealy or floury coating on the surfaces of their leaves. This protective coating, typically created by hairs or wax, is unpalatable to deer. Its presence indicates that the species, in this case *S. cineraria,* evolved where intense sun is the norm: the coating shields the leaves from damaging rays and excessive moisture loss. For gardeners this means the plant should be grown in full sun.

Dusty miller hails from the Mediterranean region and is grown for its attractive gray or silver-white felted foliage. The leaves grow from the base and are variously lobed and cut depending upon the selection. 'White Diamond' may be the most widely grown variety, but its twice-divided leaves are not as silvery as some. It grows 15 in. tall or so.

HOW TO GROW

Dusty miller thrives in poor, very well drained soil and becomes leggy and loses some of its silveryness in moist, rich soil or without enough sun. However, it is forgiving and seldom has cultural problems except with wet feet in poor-draining soil. Home gardeners mostly put out young transplants that have been started commercially from seed or cuttings. These are available in nurseries in late spring. It is wise to pinch out the growing point to encourage stocky, bushy growth. In mild winter areas, dusty miller often survives outdoors, but this is not reliable; new young plants are recommended for the best displays.

QUICK LOOK

Hardiness
Annual
Height and spread
1–2 ft. × 1 ft.
Deer resistance rating
9–10

DESIGN TIPS

A really beautiful plant, dusty miller has too often been part of a garish or unimaginative design. Public parks set out miles of it each season, usually in rows like soldiers and often as a foil for brassy marigolds or flaming red salvias. They are planted to "beautify" the entryways of drive-ins and gas stations, where the plants are often neglected and seldom look their best. However, it does indicate their toughness and toleration for urban pollution. Consider planting dusty miller in groups or even drifts with 1-ft. tall, white or pink zinnias, bronze fennel (*Foeniculum vulgare* 'Purpureum'), or shrub verbena (*Lantana camara*). Nestling at the feet of silvery Russian sage (*Perovskia*) and bluebeard (*Caryopteris* ×*clandonensis*), dusty miller looks like a white skirt. For more impact, use it with purple-leaved *Weigela* Fine Wine ('Bramwell'). Purple-leaved basil (*Ocimum basilicum* 'Dark Opal' or 'Siam Queen') is an interesting companion too, along with other dark-leaved plants. Containers and hanging baskets show off dusty miller well. Use it as a foliage companion for trailing raspberry verbena or fanflower (*Scaevola*), perhaps in a hanging basket.

'Silver Dust' probably has the most finely cut leaves. This 8- to 12-in. tall beauty has delicate leaves that present a lacelike effect. Some reports tell of 'Silver Dust' overwintering in zone 7 for several years. If it comes through the first winter, it is likely to get much taller as the plant matures. 'Cirrus' is whiter but not as lacy, with broader leaves. It grows about 8 in. tall and seldom produces flowers. For very white leaves, choose 'New Look'. The oakleaf-shaped leaves are heavily white-felted. 'Snow Storm', sometimes called 'Silver Cloud', has wide, strappy foliage.

Dusty miller hails from the Mediterranean region and is grown for its attractive gray or silver-white felted foliage.

Dusty miller (*Senecio cineraria*) makes a good edging plant.

Floss flower

Ageratum houstonianum

NATIVE TO the warm climates of Mexico and the West Indies, floss flower is popular as a late-spring, summer, and fall annual for gardens elsewhere. Its long bloom time and easy care have made it a ubiquitous selection for bedding in public parks, where unfortunately it often lacks pizzazz. When combined imaginatively in a garden setting rather than displayed in rigid, never-ending lines, floss flower comes into its own. The plants are seldom attractive to deer, perhaps due to their fuzzy flowers and rough-textured foliage.

Traditionally with lavender-blue flowers, floss flowers now come in white and various shades of pink, bluish lavender, blue, and purple. The blooms are borne in fluffy clusters grouped into showy flower heads. Colorful from late spring through summer and into fall, floss flowers succumb only to the first frost. In warm climates they bloom year-round, and they are good container subjects for winter greenhouses and sunrooms in Canada and northern regions of the United States. The hairy, heart-shaped leaves are midgreen, toothed, and wavy along the margins.

HOW TO GROW

Since transplants are frost tender, put them out in sunny, well-drained spots when the soil and weather warm up in spring. Seeds are usually started indoors several weeks before the last frost or are propagated vegetatively. Mildew can attack the plants in some climates; keep the soil evenly moist and avoid overhead watering late in the day.

QUICK LOOK

Hardiness
Annual
Height and spread
6–36 in. × 6–18 in.
Deer resistance rating
9–10

Floss flower (*Ageratum houstonianum*).

When combined imaginatively in a garden setting rather than displayed in rigid, never-ending lines, floss flower comes into its own.

DESIGN TIPS

Many cultivars, seed strains, and series are available. Compact 'Blue Blazer' and the Hawaii series (in blues, pinks, and white) only reach 6 in. tall but are among the earliest to bloom. 'Blue Danube' and 'White Danube' make uniform, 8- to 12-in. mounds blanketed with flowers. All are valuable as edgings or front-of-the -border plants but may look best in informal drifts, perhaps with hare's tail grass (*Lagurus ovatus*) to provide some movement, or interspersed with colorful annual Shirley or corn poppies. More often one sees them in skinny rows with wax begonias or sassy marigolds, combinations that lack much charm. Consider growing a broad band of floss flower at the feet of a dark evergreen hedge. In containers add silvery height and texture with dusty miller (*Senecio cineraria*). Varieties from the vegetative Artist series, in various colors, may reach 18 in. tall with a more relaxed habit. These are perfect for decorative containers alone or in combination, maybe with gray-green sage (*Salvia officinalis*), trailing licorice plant (*Helichrysum petiolare*), or butter yellow, trailing 'Primrose Jewel' nasturtium (*Tropaeolum majus*). The vigorous, 2- to 3-ft. tall 'Blue Horizon' has endeared itself to flower arrangers. Strong-stemmed with long-lasting flowers, it is excellent as filler with cut lilies, roses, and tassel flower (*Amaranthus caudatus*), for example. 'Blue Horizon', 'Florist Blue', and other taller varieties are also splendid to fill gaps in perennial beds, perhaps when oriental poppies (*Papaver orientale*) or ornamental onions (*Allium*) have disappeared or become shabby.

Licorice plant

Helichrysum petiolare

SAVVY GARDENERS have come to realize the importance of foliage plants in garden design. Shrubby licorice plant is valued both in containers and in the ground for summer displays. Deer avoid it due to its strong licorice aroma.

This South African plant comes from dry inland regions. Its trailing stems are clothed in furry, silver, heart-shaped leaves covered with hairs. These protect the leaf surface and reduce moisture loss through transpiration in hot sun. Campers in southern Africa sometimes use cut branches of licorice plant as bedding, much as pine needles and bracken are used in North America. It is also used medicinally as a remedy for bronchial ailments.

HOW TO GROW

Licorice plant is usually started from cuttings, and young plants are widely available in garden centers in spring. The frost-tender plants must not be exposed to cold weather; don't be in a hurry to set them out. In hot zones they grow year-round. They prefer very well drained soil in sun or part shade and may be susceptible to root rot if overwatered. Avoid overhead watering where the velvety leaves will not dry before nightfall; they are susceptible to mildew.

Pinch growing tips of young plants to encourage bushy growth, and don't hesitate to shorten long branches later in the season to force new shoots. They are food plants for caterpillars of painted lady, American lady, and other butterflies, but damaged plants put out more leaves after the larvae pupate.

QUICK LOOK

Hardiness
Annual
Height and spread
6–9 in. × 3 ft.
Deer resistance rating
9–10

DESIGN TIPS

A low-maintenance, drought- and heat-tolerant plant that needs no deadheading, mixes well with other plants, and has beautiful silver leaves—what's not to like? More silver than the species, the leaves of 'White Licorice' are defined with a silver rim. A variegated silver and white form, 'Variegatum', also known as 'Licorice Splash', is not as vigorous a grower but combines well, especially with white, pinks, and reds. 'Petite Licorice', or 'Minus', has more compact growth and smaller silver leaves. It is useful in window boxes and baskets where space may be tight. 'Limelight', also known as 'Aurea', has chartreuse leaves that harmonize easily, especially with yellows, reds, purple, and blues.

Hanging baskets and container designs need trailing plants to soften the rim and complete the picture. Licorice plant fills this function to a tee. Have fun with combinations such as 'Limelight' with metallic purple-leaved Persian shield (*Strobilanthes dyeriana*), purple fountain grass (*Pennisetum setaceum* 'Rubrum'), and orange zinnias. Or have licorice plant show off pink lantana with tall pink snapdragons and floss flower. Try an eye-catching window box with scarlet sage, orange zinnias, strawflowers, and 'Petite Licorice' tumbling over the edge. Licorice plant is also attractive with lavender fanflower (*Scaevola*), purple heliotrope, and Swan River daisy (*Brachycome iberidifolia*) in a basket. All of these and other combinations can just as well be planted in the landscape with shrubs and perennials where silver or chartreuse foliage can be used to buffer strong colors or light up a ho-hum corner. Look out for *Helichrysum thianschanicum* 'Icicles', which at less than 12 in. looks like a silver pine seedling.

A low-maintenance, drought- and heat-tolerant plant that needs no deadheading, mixes well with other plants, and has beautiful silver leaves—what's not to like?

Licorice plant (*Helichrysum petiolare*).

Signet marigold

Tagetes tenuifolia

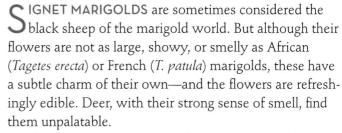

SIGNET MARIGOLDS are sometimes considered the black sheep of the marigold world. But although their flowers are not as large, showy, or smelly as African (*Tagetes erecta*) or French (*T. patula*) marigolds, these have a subtle charm of their own—and the flowers are refreshingly edible. Deer, with their strong sense of smell, find them unpalatable.

Alternate common names of Mexican marigold and bush marigold attest to this tender plant's Mexican nativity and bushy shape. It makes a mound of lacy, bright green, citrusy-scented leaves, and the 1½-in. single flowers make up in number what they lose in size. The loose informality of signet marigold fits well into most modern gardens.

HOW TO GROW

Signet marigolds are sold as transplants in garden centers. However, plants are easy to start from seed, as are other marigolds. Sow indoors a few weeks before the last frost date, or sow outdoors when the soil has warmed. Few sunny places in the garden are unsuitable for signet marigolds, except where the soil is constantly wet. Plant them at the front of beds and borders, as informal edgings, tumbling out of containers and hanging baskets, in rock gardens, or among vegetables and herbs in kitchen and herb gardens. Marigolds have long been grown as companion plants in vegetable gardens to deter pests, especially aphids. Although solid documentation of this is scarce, the cheery flowers are colorful here, and the petals are handy to garnish salads and make marigold butter (Barash 1997).

QUICK LOOK

Hardiness
Annual
Height and spread
9–18 in. × 1 ft.
Deer resistance rating
7–8

Signet marigold (*Tagetes tenuifolia*).

These marigolds
have a subtle charm
of their own—and
the flowers are
refreshingly edible.

DESIGN TIPS

Compared to French and African marigolds, there are only
a few strains and cultivars (all single-flowered) of signet
marigolds, although their blood is in many a hybrid. The
12- to 18-in. tall members of the Gem series are the most
widely grown. 'Lemon Gem' has bright yellow petals
around a darker center, while 'Golden Gem', 'Tangerine
Gem', and 'Orange Gem' are shades of orange. 'Lulu'
is a sweet, 1-ft. tall, yellow cultivar with a looser habit.
Starfire strain, 6 to 8 in. tall, is available in mixed colors.
Except to edge vegetable gardens, these heat lovers are
most attractive planted in drifts or groups. They harmonize well with apricot, orange, or purple hummingbird
mints (*Agastache*), flowering tobacco (*Nicotiana*), or blue
mealycup sage (*Salvia farinacea*), among others.

French marigolds are more formal. Their uniform 10- to
12-in. height makes them perfect as edging plants or for
a living picture design (carpet bedding). Double or single
golf-ball-sized flowers come in the yellow, orange, reddish brown range, often striped. The semidouble Durango
series blooms in multiple color combinations. The Bounty
series does especially well in hot climates. Named cultivars abound.

The African, or tall, types may reach 3 to 4 ft. high,
good candidates for the back of the border or for cutting.
Colors range from creamy white to all shades of yellow
and orange. The solitary, mostly double flowers sit like
large tennis balls atop tall stems. The Lady series stands
some 3 to 4 ft. tall and includes primrose as well as the
usual colors. The 2- to 3-ft. Gold Coin series comes in yellow and light orange.

Perennials

The forget-me-not flowers of Siberian bugloss (*Brunnera macrophylla*) and common bleeding heart (*Dicentra spectabilis*) combine to create this pink and blue spring display.

Azure monkshood

Aconitum carmichaelii

ELEGANT SPIKES of dark blue flowers make azure monkshood a welcome sight in late summer and fall, when the garden often has a lull. Its strong upright stems are clothed with glossy, dark green leaves cut into three or five lobes. Reddish fall color often accompanies the last blooms in fall. Other species, such as dark blue common monkshood (*Aconitum napellus*) and its white- and pink-flowered cultivars, and yellow wolfsbane (*A. lamarkii*), also enliven gardens at that time.

Monkshoods are underused garden perennials, perhaps due to their historical association with evil. Legends abound from mythology and down through the ages, telling of murders and suicides as well as monkshood's common use by witches in the making of love potions. All parts of these plants, especially the roots, are poisonous to ingest, even for deer—a strong attribute for our gardens. The roots were once used as poison bait, hence alternate common names like wolfsbane, tiger bane, and leopard's bane. Others, including helmet flower, friar's cap, and Turk's cap, refer to the unusual hooded flowers, shaped like Roman helmets. The handsome leaves are mostly deeply cut.

HOW TO GROW

Low-maintenance monkshoods are easy to grow in sun or light shade where the soil is rich and remains consistently moist. They seldom need to be staked, as the flower stems are strong enough to support themselves, but a site protected from strong wind is wise. Deadheading the lead spike to its base after it fades encourages lateral branching. To increase stock, divide the tuberous roots in fall, being careful not to get sap on your skin. Plant the divisions in a spot where they will be undisturbed for many

QUICK LOOK

Hardiness
Zones 3–7
Height and spread
2–3 ft. × 1½ ft.
Deer resistance rating
9–10

'Arendsii' azure monkshood (*Aconitum carmichaelii* 'Arendsii'). Photo by judywhite/GardenPhotos.com.

years. Collect seed after the pods have dried on the plant, and sow directly outdoors.

When working around monkshoods, be extremely careful not to get sap in an open cut or in the eyes—gloves are always recommended. Never plant them near vegetable gardens or children's play areas, or where their roots, flowers, buds, or foliage could be mistaken for another plant such as related delphiniums. Pretty though they may be, the flowers are *not* acceptable for garnishing salads or dinner dishes.

DESIGN TIPS

Perhaps the best monkshood for late bloom, 4-ft. tall 'Arendsii' azure monkshood is a winner for its leathery leaves, erect habit, and stout clusters of pale blue flowers, which are violet inside and glow at dusk as if lit from within. Monkshoods are striking companions in perennial and mixed borders, especially those not in full sun. Their vertical habit is a perfect contrast to the roundness of *Coreopsis*, hardy geraniums, and milkweeds, for example, and they are eye-catching growing among Thunberg bush clover (*Lespedeza thunbergii*), glossy abelia (*Abelia* ×*grandiflora*), and native summersweet (*Clethra alnifolia*) in shrub collections. Sometimes the lower stems of monkshoods become bare and ugly. If this is a problem, either grow them through a deer-resistant groundcover such as deadnettle (*Lamium*) or autumn fern (*Dryopteris erythrosora*), or plant a carpet of autumn crocus (*Colchicum*) at their feet for the following year.

Earlier-blooming monkshoods include bicolor monkshood (*Aconitum* ×*cammarum*), a group of hybrids that bear spikes of variously colored flowers. Popular cultivars include 2- to 3-ft. tall 'Blue Sceptre' (blue and white), strong-stemmed, upright 'Bressingham Spire' (violet), and 4-ft. tall 'Newry Blue' (navy blue). Creamy white 'Ivorine' blooms in late spring above a mound of deeply lobed leaves. Partner it with hybrid sages (*Salvia* ×*sylvestris*) such as 'May Night' ('Mainacht'), 'Rose Queen', or 'Blue Mound' ('Blauhugel').

Elegant spikes of dark blue flowers make azure monkshood a welcome sight in late summer and fall, when the garden often has a lull.

Bigroot geranium

Geranium macrorrhizum

SOUTHERN EUROPEAN bigroot geranium, also known as scented cranesbill, belongs to the large and valuable group of hardy geraniums that are so much a part of perennial gardens. Tough and vigorous, this species has thick, fleshy rhizomes that spread politely and seldom become a nuisance. The soft, fuzzy, light green leaves are deeply divided into seven- or eight-lobed segments and may reach 8 in. across. In fall they turn lovely shades of red, deep rose, and yellow unless it is too shady; in mild climates they remain evergreen. Dense clusters of 1-in. magenta flowers with dark red sepals bloom in late spring. The scent (pleasant? unpleasant? it depends upon your nose) emitted when any part of the plant is bruised is pungent, causing deer to largely avoid it. In Bulgaria bigroot geranium is raised to extract zdravets ("health") oil, used in skin care products, perfumery, and aromatherapy. In the past it was grown to produce oil of geranium.

HOW TO GROW
Plant bigroot geranium in sun or light shade in average humus-rich soil that drains well. Apply organic mulch in summer, especially where the soil tends to be dry. It is quite tolerant of most soil types and succeeds in dry shade where other perennials fail. Set plants 18 in. apart, closer for a groundcover. They will spread gently and grow together in a couple of years; break off pieces of root to control if necessary.

DESIGN TIPS
Cultivars include pale pink 'Ingwerson's Variety', compact 10-in. tall 'Bevan's Variety', and white-flowered 'Album'

QUICK LOOK

Hardiness
Zones 3–8
Height and spread
1–2 ft. × 1–3 ft.
Deer resistance rating
8–10

with contrasting pink sepals. 'Variegatum', with cream-spotted grayish green foliage, is not as robust.

As a low-maintenance groundcover, bigroot geranium is ideal among trees and shrubs or in mixed borders. It is charming beneath silverbells (*Halesia*), shadbush (*Amelanchier*), and deutzias (*Deutzia*), for example. Plant 'Ingwerson's Variety' beneath pink weigela or beautybush (*Kolkwitzia*) as a color echo. It does well even at the dry base of wintergreen barberry (*Berberis julianae*) and other hedges; consider a planting beneath tall oaks, beeches, and maples. On the edge of woodlands and in lightly shaded borders, bigroot geranium is great in front of perennials such as bluestar (*Amsonia*), false indigo (*Baptisia*), and columbines (*Aquilegia*). It blends well, too, with barrenwort (*Epimedium*), hellebores (*Helleborus*), and lady's mantle (*Alchemilla*). Tall purple-pink or white foxgloves (*Digitalis*) rising from a mass of bigroot geranium is unforgettable. The handsome foliage contrasts well with that of astilbes and ferns in light shade, where bigroot geranium might take the place of deer-attracting hostas. Where there is more sun, try silvery lamb's ears (*Stachys byzantina*) and wormwoods (*Artemisia*) as companions.

Deer avoid many other hardy geraniums, although there are reports of Endress's geranium (*Geranium endressii*) being seriously browsed. Purplish pink Cambridge geranium (*G.* ×*cantabrigiense*) and its cultivars—spreading, pink-tinged white 'Biokovo' and 9-in. tall, deep red 'Karmina'—are excellent for edging paths or at the front of flower borders. 'Rozanne' hardy geranium (*G.* 'Rozanne'), selected in 2008 as Perennial Plant of the Year by the Perennial Plant Association, is another winner with scented leaves that deer spurn. Its mounding plants are covered with 2-in., white-eyed, violet-blue flowers from late spring through hard frost.

As a low-maintenance groundcover, bigroot geranium is ideal among trees and shrubs or in mixed borders.

Bigroot geranium 'Album' (*Geranium macrorrhizum* 'Album').

Black snakeroot

Actaea racemosa

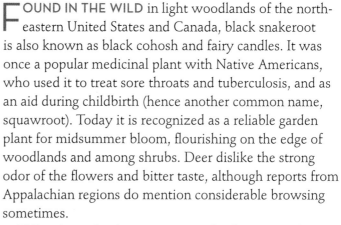

QUICK LOOK

Hardiness
Zones 3–7
Height and spread
6–8 ft. × 3–4 ft.
Deer resistance rating
7–9

Black snakeroot (*Actaea racemosa*).

FOUND IN THE WILD in light woodlands of the north-eastern United States and Canada, black snakeroot is also known as black cohosh and fairy candles. It was once a popular medicinal plant with Native Americans, who used it to treat sore throats and tuberculosis, and as an aid during childbirth (hence another common name, squawroot). Today it is recognized as a reliable garden plant for midsummer bloom, flourishing on the edge of woodlands and among shrubs. Deer dislike the strong odor of the flowers and bitter taste, although reports from Appalachian regions do mention considerable browsing sometimes.

Tall and stately, *Actaea racemosa*, also known as *Cimicifuga racemosa*, has wiry, dark, branched stems clothed with deeply cut, toothed leaves. In midsummer the stems are topped with tapering, 2-ft. long bottlebrush spikes of flowers. Like little pearls when in bud, they open to tiny creamy flowers, fluffy with stamens. Some call these malodorous, others fragrant, but they attract butterflies and hosts of other insects. After the flowers fade, small green spheres (seed capsules) follow, turn brown, and stay on the plant through the winter.

HOW TO GROW

Black snakeroot requires little maintenance. However, it is often slow to establish, sometimes taking two or three seasons to bloom. The roots resent disturbance, so plant it in a partly shaded spot where it is unlikely to be disturbed. It is best in humus-rich soil that is well drained but remains damp. Apply a summer mulch of compost or other organic material to help maintain soil moisture. If the plant is stressed for water, the leaves become crispy

along the edges. Propagate by division of well-established plants in spring.

DESIGN TIPS

If you are looking for a vertical accent in a woodland or partly shaded garden, black snakeroot is a good candidate. Its attractive divided leaves provide texture and remain handsome throughout the season. Plant groups of three or five for best effect, as bugbanes are slow to bulk up and may take two or three years to give their best. Although they tolerate full sun in northern gardens, they may be most dramatic in lightly shaded gardens backed by dark-leaved shrubs or woodland. Boxwoods, Japanese plum yew (*Cephalotaxus harringtonia*, zones 6 to 9), and Japanese andromeda (*Pieris japonica*) are valuable companions, as are tall ostrich fern (*Matteuccia struthiopteris*) and royal fern (*Osmunda regalis*). Other notable species include earlier-blooming native American or mountain bugbane (*Actaea podocarpa*), with similar white flowers on mostly branching 4-ft. tall stems. This species is ideal for shaded native plant or meadow gardens, perhaps with fragrant sumac (*Rhus aromatica*), spicebush, or summersweet. The latest to bloom is Russian kamchatka bugbane (*Actaea simplex*). Several cultivars are superior to the species. In late fall 'White Pearl' bears crowded 2-ft. long spikes of flowers. Its leaves resist crisping in southern gardens, where yaupon holly (*Ilex vomitoria*) is a good companion. 'James Compton' is more compact, seldom topping 3 ft. tall. Its bronzy purple leaves tolerate full sun in northern climes. 'Brunette' and 'Hillside Black Beauty' are also good dark-leaved cultivars.

Tall wands of snakeroot flowers add valuable height and interest to flower arrangements, too.

Its attractive divided leaves provide texture and remain handsome throughout the season.

Blue false indigo

Baptisia australis

LOW-MAINTENANCE, tolerant of drought and heat, almost pest and disease free, seldom needs staking or division—what more could any gardener ask of a plant? Blue false indigo is truly a workhorse. This native of the eastern United States pushes its blue-green shoots skywards in late spring, followed by lupinelike spikes of blue pea flowers that appear in early summer. Native Americans valued blue false indigo for its antiseptic properties, but early settlers used it as a rather poor source of blue dye (*bapto* means "to dip or dye"). The specific name *australis* refers to its southern range rather than to Australia. Quaint common names such as rattlebush (its rattling black seedpods were sometimes used to amuse babies) and horsefly weed (recalling the practice of attaching branches to horse tack to keep off flies) indicate its widespread familiarity. Some parts of the plant, notably the seeds, are poisonous to deer, which avoid it.

HOW TO GROW

For best results, plant in a sunny spot in well-drained but not overly rich soil. Plants in partly shaded spots tend to bloom less and have weaker stems that may need support. When established, usually two to three years, the taproots push deep, and plants seek out water from way down. This enables them to survive and even thrive during dry periods, but makes it difficult to divide mature clumps. Choose the spot for new plantings carefully. Start seeds in pots (chip or file the hard seed coat prior to seeding) so that there is a minimum of root disturbance at planting-out time.

QUICK LOOK

Hardiness
Zones 3–9
Height and spread
3–4 ft. × 3–4 ft.
Deer resistance rating
8–10

DESIGN TIPS

Blue false indigo is a standout alone, massed as a hedge, or in small groups. It mixes well in the deer-tolerant spring garden as well as later in the year. Try it beside a drift of late yellow or white narcissus, such as *Narcissus* 'Stratosphere', *N. poeticus* var. *recurvatus*, or *N.* 'Pay Day'. Several false indigo hybrids are available. Late-May-blooming 'Purple Smoke', with charcoal stems bearing dusty purple flowers, is popular as a specimen plant that contrasts stunningly with pale pink peonies or orange oriental poppies. Other hybrids, from the North Carolina Botanical Garden and Chicago Botanic Garden breeding programs, include yellow-flowered 'Carolina Moonlight', 'Screaming Yellow', and 'Solar Flare Prairieblues'. *Baptisia lactea*, *B. leucantha*, and *B. alba* are white-blooming species, superb in white gardens. Early-blooming 'Wayne's World', a selection of *B. alba*, bears 18-in. long spikes of white flowers on 4-ft. tall plants. After bloom time, some gardeners utilize the clean blue-green foliage and sturdy habit of blue false indigo, clipping the plants into rounded shapes (sacrificing the inflated green seedpods that mature to black rattles) as temporary topiary. This is an interesting foil for later-blooming yarrows (*Achillea*), butterfly weed (*Asclepias tuberosa*), and Russian sage (*Perovskia*), for example in beds and borders. Many of the tall, late-blooming salvias are good companions too, although where frost comes early, they may not bloom before being cut down. Fresh-cut flowers and dried seedpods of blue false indigo are decorative indoors.

It pushes its blue-green shoots skywards in late spring, followed by lupinelike spikes of blue pea flowers that appear in early summer.

Blue false indigo (*Baptisia australis*).

Cushion spurge

Euphorbia polychroma

THE GENUS *Euphorbia* includes some 2000 or more plants, all of which are more or less ignored by deer. Most have an irritating milky sap that is unpalatable to mammals and may cause dermatitis in certain people. The diverse members range from shrubby Christmas poinsettias (*E. pulcherrima*) to succulent treelike forms found in Africa (*E. tetragona*). Some (*E. pseudocactus*) are mistaken for cactus, a family native only in the New World.

Euphorbia polychroma, also known as *E. epithymoides*, is one of the springtime stars of the garden. It makes neat, rounded mounds of light green, leafy stems topped in spring by chartreuse "flowers," which consist of clusters of insignificant true flowers surrounded by small, acid yellow bracts. Bloom time is long, and afterwards the foliage remains handsome, often producing some color in the fall.

HOW TO GROW

Plant cushion spurge in light shade; full sun is fine in the North, but in intense southern sun plants may become leggy and lose their compact habit. Average well-drained soil is sufficient; they tolerate drought conditions well. Deadhead before seedpods develop to avoid self-seeding. After flowering has finished, cut plants back by about a third, and bushy new growth will carry them through the season. When working around euphorbias, protect yourself by wearing gloves and avoiding contact with your face or other exposed skin in case of a dermatological reaction. Do not get the sap in your eyes.

DESIGN TIPS

Mixed borders are eminently suitable for cushion spurge. Plant it toward the front along with silver-leaved worm-

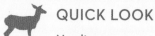

QUICK LOOK

Hardiness
Zones 4–8
Height and spread
12–18 in. × 18 in.
Deer resistance rating
9–10

'Bonfire' cushion spurge (*Euphorbia polychroma* 'Bonfire').

Bloom time is long, and afterwards the foliage remains handsome, often producing some color in the fall.

wood (*Artemisia* 'Powis Castle'), rainbow-hued German and blue Siberian iris (*Iris* ×*germanica* and *I. sibirica*), hybrid sage (*Salvia* ×*sylvestris*), and poppies. It provides a foil for the late-to-leaf, shrubby Russian sage (*Perovskia*) and bluebeard (*Caryopteris*). Spring-blooming shrubs such as yellow kerria (*Kerria japonica*) and orange Japanese flowering quince (*Chaenomeles japonica*) look wonderful with a bright underplanting of cushion spurge. In cottage gardens, plant it with blue false indigo (*Baptisia australis*), larkspur (*Consolida ajacis*), Shirley poppies (*Papaver rhoeas*), and crimson or orange wallflowers (*Erysimum*). 'Bonfire' is a particular favorite. Its soft, almost furry, new foliage is bronzy to burgundy in vibrant contrast to its chartreuse flowers. The foliage color remains all season, contrasting well with silver-leaved lamb's ears (*Stachys byzantina*), lavender cotton (*Santolina chamaecyparissus*), and *Artemisia* 'Silver Mound'. 'First Blush' has rosy pink young foliage that becomes green, edged with pinkish white; in fall it turns red. Lovely, variegated 'Helena's Blush' wood spurge (*Euphorbia amygdaloides* 'Helena's Blush') has green and cream leaves with hints of pink beneath. Unfortunately it is not as robust as 'Efanthia', an upright, 2-ft. evergreen with bronze young growth and strong fall color.

Other superior herbaceous species include orange Griffith's spurge (*Euphorbia griffithii*), *E. dulcis* (especially purple-leaved 'Chameleon'), and trailing, evergreen myrtle spurge (*E. myrsinites*). With its dense spirals of blue-green leaves and brilliant yellow bracts in spring, myrtle spurge excels tumbling over rocks or walls. After bloom time, cut all the flowered stems back hard to the crown to force fresh bluish growth. Many of these spurges are ideal for container plantings, either alone or in combinations. Beware of cypress spurge (*E. cyparissias*), which is a stoloniferous thug under decent conditions, though useful for dry, difficult areas.

Fringed bleeding heart

Dicentra eximia

EASY-TO-GROW, long-blooming fringed bleeding heart is a workhorse in shady gardens. It is native to woodlands and rocky outcrops in the eastern United States and Canada. Pacific bleeding heart (*Dicentra formosa*), wild from British Columbia to California, is showier, but together these two species have spawned several superior hybrids. Bloom begins in spring and in temperate gardens often continues well into fall. The locketlike flowers are similar to those of common bleeding heart (*D. spectabilis*), but the plants are lower growing and bloom repeatedly through the season. Their ferny foliage remains good-looking through summer heat. Deer avoid bleeding hearts due to their poisonous sap.

Mounds of gray-green (sometimes bluish), deeply cut leaves and arching, succulent flower stems arise from the base. Several heart-shaped flowers in shades of pink, red, or white dangle from each stalk. Their nectar attracts hummingbirds.

HOW TO GROW

Clump-forming, perennial fringed bleeding heart enjoys a cool root run but needs good drainage, especially in winter. A lightly or partly shaded spot is ideal—avoid intense sun, especially in the South. Fertile, well-drained soil is best, with plenty of organic matter to retain summer moisture. The plants grow from a scaly rootstock. Ants distribute the seeds and spread them freely (unless the plants are deadheaded), sometimes resulting in large stands. The western species withstands drought better than the eastern one but is not as tolerant of summer heat and humidity. The hybrids and named cultivars rarely come true from seed and must be propagated vegeta-

QUICK LOOK

Hardiness
Zones 3–9
Height and spread
1–2 ft. × 18 in.
Deer resistance rating
9–10

tively. Divide clumps in fall or take 3- to 4-in. long root cuttings in summer or fall.

DESIGN TIPS

Fringed bleeding hearts look great in shady rock gardens nestling against boulders or outcroppings. Where space is limited, select smaller cultivars such as pure white 'Sweetheart', deep rosy red 'Zestful', or deep pink 'Stuart Boothman'; all grow about 12 in. tall. Mix them with moss pink (*Phlox subulata*), columbines (*Aquilegia*), and barrenworts (*Epimedium*) for a great spring display. The silver-marked foliage of lungworts (*Pulmonaria*) provides good contrast all season, especially with white-flowered 'Alba' or 'Snowdrift'. In light woodlands and shaded borders, good companions for dusky red 'Bacchanal' and rosy red 'Bountiful' include Siberian squills (*Scilla sibirica*), coral bells (*Heuchera*), lady's mantle (*Alchemilla*), and bigroot geranium (*Geranium macrorrhizum*). For later bloom consider goatsbeard (*Aruncus dioicus*), monkshood (*Aconitum*), autumn crocus (*Colchicum*), and meadow rues (*Thalictrum*). Astilbes and ferns work well too, but if their leaves do not contrast sufficiently for your taste, try Japanese painted fern, which plays off well against the blue-green foliage of red-flowered 'Luxuriant' or white 'Langtrees'. In native plant or wildflower gardens, grow fringed bleeding heart with black snakeroot (*Actaea racemosa*), wild geranium (*Geranium maculatum*), blue flag (*Iris versicolor*), and heart-leaved golden Alexander (*Zizia aptera*). In mixed borders any of the many selections of fringed bleeding heart are attractive contrasted with Japanese skimmia (*Skimmia japonica*), boxwood (*Buxus*), and Russian cypress (*Microbiota decussata*).

Long-favored common bleeding heart (*Dicentra spectabilis*) still has a place in many gardens and in people's hearts. Contrary to the light green leaves of the species, 'Gold Heart' has bright yellow leaves that hold their color.

Its ferny foliage remains good-looking through summer heat.

Fringed bleeding heart (*Dicentra eximia*).

Hybrid astilbe

Astilbe ×arendsii

THE FEATHERY flower plumes of hybrid astilbe are always an arresting sight massed in lightly shaded gardens. The bulk of astilbes in the marketplace are hybrids, lumped under *Astilbe ×arendsii*; their parentage includes several species, particularly *A. chinensis* var. *davidii*, *A. japonica*, and *A. thunbergii*, known collectively as false spireas or just astilbes. Some are also cultivars of the species themselves, including star astilbe (*A. simplicifolia* 'Bronze Elegance') and Chinese astilbe (*A. chinensis* 'Visions'), a plant enhanced by its special fragrance. Deer apparently don't like the fernlike texture of astilbe leaves.

HOW TO GROW

Long-lived hybrid astilbes thrive where the soil is moist, deep, and high in humus. The addition of plenty of compost or other organic material at planting time, followed by an annual top dressing, is beneficial to reduce water loss from the soil. Avoid planting in full sun in hot regions; where summers are cooler, these plants often thrive in full sun. If the roots dry out, the leaves shrivel along the edges as a sign of stress. Maintenance is low: staking, dividing, and spraying for pests and diseases are seldom necessary. After the flowers have faded, allow them to remain on the plants to provide decorative value well into winter. The rusty-colored dried plumes catch falling snow and become encrusted with frost on chilly mornings. If division becomes necessary to increase stock, lift the whole clump and take young pieces from the outside to grow on. The inner woody centers can be discarded, as it will take a machete or saw to cut them apart.

QUICK LOOK

Hardiness
Zones 4–8
Height and spread
1–4 ft. × 2 ft.
Deer resistance rating
7–9

A partly shaded bed containing cultivars of hybrid astilbe (*Astilbe ×arendsii*).

The rusty-colored dried plumes catch falling snow and become encrusted with frost on chilly mornings.

DESIGN TIPS

The bloom time (early to late summer) and height of astilbes vary by species and cultivar. Flower plumes may be dense and tight or loose and feathery, but all are borne on upright, wiry stems. Colors range from pure white ('Snowdrift') through creamy white ('Deutschland'), pink ('Bressingham Pink'), and orchid ('Cattleya'), to salmon ('Vesuvius'), dark red ('Etna', 'Fanal'), and carmine red ('Federsee'). The blooms make long-lasting cut flowers; harvest when half-open.

Astilbes are especially valuable massed in the landscape as tall groundcovers, perhaps under high trees. In light shade they combine well with ferns, barrenworts, hellebores, and Hakone grass. Instead of planting the customary combination with deer-attracting hostas, substitute less susceptible Rodgers' flower (*Rodgersia*) or bigleaf goldenray (*Ligularia dentata*). Some gardeners ring hostas with astilbes to try to fool the deer—they are not fools. Other shade-loving groundcover plants also combine well—lungwort (*Pulmonaria*), leadwort (*Ceratostigma plumbaginoides*), and deadnettle (*Lamium*) come to mind. The dark green or reddish ferny foliage of astilbes is an attractive foil for ubiquitous groundcovers such as *Vinca major* and greedy Japanese pachysandra (*Pachysandra terminalis*). Decide if your soil is sufficiently rich to accommodate the latter plus astilbe. Astilbes are equally successful in wet places where their tenacious roots ease soil erosion; combine them with cinnamon fern or other ferns beside ponds and streams. For impact in beds or borders, plant astilbes in groups of at least three. They partner especially well with blue false indigo, meadow rues, fringed bleeding heart, and lady's mantle.

Hybrid sage

Salvia ×sylvestris

THE HUGE SAGE CLAN includes a host of superior ornamentals as well as familiar culinary herbs. Hybrid sage is a result of a garden cross between woodland sage (*Salvia nemorosa*) and meadow sage (*S. pratensis*). Subsequent breeding has resulted in *S. ×superba*, and various cultivars are listed under either Latin name. By any name these handsome, easy-to-grow, clumping perennials with strong vertical spikes of vivid flowers have a place in most gardens. Butterflies and hummingbirds are attracted to the flowers, while deer are repelled by the aromatic foliage.

'May Night' ('Mainacht'), named Perennial Plant of the Year by the Perennial Plant Association in 1997, is among the best of the widely grown hybrid sage cultivars. Its branched, 18-in. stems are clothed with wrinkled, gray-green leaves and long-lasting, dense spikes of dark violet-blue flowers. Similar 'East Friesland' ('Ostfriesland') bears dazzling purple-violet flower spikes; 'Lubecca' may reach 30 in. tall.

HOW TO GROW
For best results, plant hybrid sages in well-drained, fertile soil in full sun. They tolerate very light shade, but stems tend to be weak and plants often require staking. Once established, the plants tolerate drought well, but prefer to have a regular supply of moisture. Deadheading to the base of the primary spike after bloom encourages a second crop of flowers. Increase these hardy perennials by division in early spring or root cuttings of young shoots.

DESIGN TIPS
Mass hybrid sages in formal beds, perhaps with bright yellow 'Zagreb' threadleaf coreopsis (*Coreopsis verticil-*

QUICK LOOK

Hardiness
Zones 4–9
Height and spread
2–3 ft. × 1 ft.
Deer resistance rating
9–10

lata 'Zagreb'), pink *Dianthus* 'Firewitch', and blue-violet 'Rozanne' hardy geranium (*Geranium* 'Rozanne'). In rock gardens 'May Night' provides height for cushion and trailing alpines such as low stonecrops (*Sedum acre*) and pussytoes (*Antennaria*). Plant them in mixed borders and planters where their neat, upright habit is an asset. 'Blue Hill' blooms for a long time with true blue flowers. Floriferous, 30-in. tall 'Rose Queen' ('Rosakoenigin') bears rose flowers, lovely with irises and Jupiter's beard or valerian (*Centranthus ruber* var. *coccineus*).

With the popularity of "temperennials" (tender perennials), many South American and Mexican sages have come on the market, usually hardy in zones 7 to 10, but flowered as summer annuals elsewhere. Most are late blooming, better for southern gardens rather than for those with early frost. Anise sage (*Salvia guaranitica*) 'Black and Blue' is a shrublike monster that sometimes reaches 6 ft. tall; it is excellent as a loose hedge. Show off its intensely dark flowers against the golden fall foliage of Arkansas blue star (*Amsonia hubrichtii*), large grasses, or 'Coronation Gold' yarrow (*Achillea* 'Coronation Gold'). In fall, southeastern azure sage (*S. azurea*, zones 5 to 9) has the most glorious sky blue flowers. Though somewhat ungainly in habit, at 4 ft. tall it is well suited to informal meadow or native plant gardens and tolerates heat and humidity well. Late-summer Mexican bush sage (*S. leucantha*) has tall, shrubby stems topped with furry purple spikes of white flowers. Hummingbirds love it.

These handsome, easy-to-grow, clumping perennials with strong vertical spikes of vivid flowers have a place in most gardens.

'May Night' hybrid sage (*Salvia* ×*sylvestris* 'May Night').

Japanese spurge

Pachysandra terminalis

JAPANESE SPURGE, often simply called pachysandra, remains one of the most popular groundcover plants. This greedy, spreading evergreen has compressed whorls of alternate, dark green, glossy leaves at the tips of thick, upright stems. In spring, terminal spikes of small white or pinkish flowers appear. It colonizes fast by means of aggressive rhizomes. Deer ignore it perhaps due to its odor and leathery foliage, or for fear of tripping among the dense myriad of stems.

HOW TO GROW

As a groundcover, plant Japanese spurge 6 to 12 in. apart in light or full shade. Too much sun may cause the foliage to bleach out, especially in southern gardens. It does best in humus-rich, well-drained soil that remains moist in summer. A real survivor, Japanese spurge fights for water and nutrients when planted beneath shallow-rooted trees (beech, maple, and so forth). In places where the soil is not welcoming, be sure to prepare it thoroughly prior to planting; keep new plants well watered and mulched until established. Japanese spurge is too greedy to sustain spring bulbs among the plants for more than a season or two. Pests and diseases seldom bother this low-maintenance plant. Propagate by dividing the plants in spring or fall.

DESIGN TIPS

As a groundcover for shade, Japanese spurge has no equal. Often it is the only plant to tolerate deep shade and difficult areas, and it is perfect for those circumstances. Japanese spurge is the best plant to colonize the base of tall deciduous trees, especially those where other plants

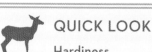

QUICK LOOK

Hardiness
Zones 4–9
Height and spread
9–12 in. × 18 in.
Deer resistance rating
9–10

A manicured bed of Japanese spurge (*Pachysandra terminalis*).

fail or struggle at best. It will even grow well under black walnut (*Juglans nigra*), an impossible site for many species. On rough, shaded banks where grass will not thrive and erosion is a problem, the roots of Japanese spurge grow deep and reduce the effects of heavy rains. Its low maintenance is an added bonus, since it requires neither mowing nor pruning. Another ideal place for Japanese spurge is along narrow, difficult-to-mow edges of shaded pathways. Its evergreen foliage fits as well in formal areas as in woodlands.

While the species is too aggressive for mixed borders, green and white 'Variegata' is less hostile. Its attractive, white-edged leaves brighten up shady spots under small trees and shrubs. 'Silveredge' is similar. Plant either with white-flowered sweet woodruff (*Galium odoratum*), foamflower (*Tiarella*), and bigroot geranium (*Geranium macrorrhizum*) for an interesting foliage combination. Shiny-leaved 'Green Sheen' and compact, dark green 'Green Carpet' are popular, readily available cultivars that are especially valuable in winter landscapes.

American native Allegheny spurge (*Pachysandra procumbens*) is a semievergreen clumper that does not spread. Young foliage is gray-green, sometimes mottled with brown. Pinkish white flower spikes nestle in the leaf axils in spring. This spurge is valuable in wild and native plant gardens where its controlled habit is an asset. Its fragrant, bottlebrush-like blooms provide early color and nectar for foraging insects. Cultivars include 'Eco Treasure', which has stronger leaf mottling; miniature, 4-in. tall 'Pixie', great for small containers and troughs; and unmottled 'Forest Green'.

As a groundcover for shade, Japanese spurge has no equal.

Lady's mantle

Alchemilla mollis

LADY'S MANTLE is a workhorse in the garden. Its softly hairy, rounded, toothed and scalloped leaves look good all season; in late winter tiny new leaves appear, silvery soft with hairs, then expand quickly on elongating stems. In early morning or after a shower, droplets of dew or rain collect at the base and glisten like pearls in the sunshine. In spring multitudes of small chartreuse flowers in frothy sprays appear well above the leaves. The hairy leaves deter deer from browsing.

This species is sometimes confused with less hairy common lady's mantle (*Alchemilla vulgaris*), and plants sold under this name are often mislabeled. Diminutive mountain lady's mantle (*A. alpina*) and red-stemmed lady's mantle (*A. erythropoda*) are the best other species in cultivation.

HOW TO GROW

In areas with cool summers, lady's mantle thrives in part sun or light shade. Although not as happy in warm climates, they tolerate heat if kept moist and are not fried by noonday sun. Plant about 2 ft. apart in average fertile soil that drains well, but never allow these plants to dry out. They resent summer drought; a mulch in summer is beneficial. Divide plants in early spring or start young plants from seed. Maintenance is low, except for shearing to control self-seeding. If plants look tired after bloom time, cut them back almost to the crown; within a few weeks beautiful new leaves will appear. Cut shabby individual leaves to the crown. Rejuvenate old woody plants by division, saving only the outer young growth.

QUICK LOOK

Hardiness
Zones 3–8
Height and spread
1–2 ft. × 1½ ft.
Deer resistance rating
8–9

DESIGN TIPS

This clumping perennial is valuable in the garden as an edging plant at the front of a border, or grouped as a skirt for shrubs. It is also effective massed as a groundcover in lightly shaded shrub borders, on the edge of woodlands, or under high pruned deciduous trees, perhaps mixed with naturalized sheets of blue forget-me-nots (*Myosotis*). Smaller species such as red-stemmed lady's mantle and mountain lady's mantle are suitable for rock gardens, along with moss pink (*Phlox subulata*), Turkestan onion (*Allium karataviense*), and striped bloody cranesbill (*Geranium sanguineum* var. *striatum*). The beautiful scalloped foliage of lady's mantle enhances almost any planting. Fritillarias, daffodils, grape hyacinths (*Muscari*), and other deer-resistant spring bulbs are charming partners. Interesting companions in light shade include barrenworts (*Epimedium*), astilbes, bigroot geranium (*Geranium macrorrhizum*), and ferns such as Christmas fern (*Polystichum acrostichoides*) and wood ferns (*Dryopteris*). In open borders that receive less than full-day sun, lady's mantle is elegant at the feet of Siberian iris (*Iris sibirica*), foxgloves (*Digitalis*), and monkshood (*Aconitum*), hiding any ugly "ankles" of these plants. To camouflage unattractive, browning foliage of late-spring- and summer-blooming ornamental onions (*Allium christophii*, *A. sphaerocephalon*, and *A. giganteum*, for example), plant groups of lovely lady's mantle at their feet. The effervescent sprays of small, green or yellowish green lady's mantle flowers are airy fillers for spring flower arrangements and can be dried for winter use. The attractive lobed leaves are often cut and used as a foil for bold, more formal flowers in summer and fall.

In early morning or after a shower, droplets of dew or rain collect at the base and glisten like pearls in the sunshine.

Lady's mantle in bloom (*Alchemilla mollis*).

Lenten rose

Helleborus orientalis

THE POPULARITY of hellebores is partly due to their usual resistance to deer browsing. They also produce enchanting blooms very early in the year (February or March in zone 6, when flowers are at a premium); have handsome, dark green, sometimes mottled leaves; tolerate dry conditions with aplomb; and make long-lasting cut flowers. What more could you ask?

Most of the Lenten roses on the market are hybrids. Typically the nodding, cup-shaped flowers, several per stem, are white, pink, or purple, often dappled with maroon or purple. The showy parts are actually sepals; small, deciduous nectaries replace the petals. The sepals remain good-looking for several months, attracting attention well into late spring. The long-stemmed, semievergreen, leathery leaves are hand-shaped. Several named strains are available, including Royal Heritage strain, Brandywine strain, and Mardi Gras series.

HOW TO GROW

For best results, plant hellebores in light shade in humus-rich, lightly acid to alkaline, well-drained soil that seldom dries out. However, they tolerate less-than-ideal conditions well once established; in dry shade extra organic material and a summer mulch are helpful. Under maples and other surface-rooting trees, additional water is critical during summer droughts. Set out plants 15 to 18 in. apart in fall or spring and keep well watered. Hellebores are greedy feeders; mulch in fall with decomposed leaves or compost. Remove winter-damaged leaves in early spring. Young, bright green foliage emerges just after the flowers. The plants bulk up after a few years but do not spread.

QUICK LOOK

Hardiness
Zones 4–9
Height and spread
15–18 in. × 15–18 in.
Deer resistance rating
9–10

Lenten rose (*Helleborus orientalis*).

They self-seed generously; seed takes several years to reach blooming size.

DESIGN TIPS

A drift or mass planting of Lenten roses under oaks or hickory in early spring is a special sight, especially when combined with other woodlanders such as barrenworts (*Epimedium*) and native ferns. Small trees and shrubs, including dogwoods (*Cornus*) and silverbells (*Halesia*), are enhanced by a groundcover beneath them, and the Lenten roses benefit from the shade cast when the trees leaf out. Plant Lenten roses along a shady pathway or along the north side of the house to brighten any early spring day, perhaps in combination with cheerful 'Tête-à-tête' daffodils and glory-of-the-snow (*Chionodoxa*). Spring bulbs are also great companions in flowerbeds and mixed borders. Daffodils and narcissus, fritillarias, snowdrops (*Galanthus*), and Siberian squills (*Scilla sibirica*) are especially suitable. White 'Mt. Hood' daffodils beside white Lenten roses with glory-of-the-snow beneath makes a stunning vignette. The bold leaves of hellebores are a valuable substitute for deer-attracting hostas in foliage tapestries with astilbes, meadow rues (*Thalictrum*), tall ferns, and bugbanes (*Actaea*).

Other *Helleborus* species and hybrids are worth growing. The nodding green bells of bear's foot hellebore (*H. foetidus*, zones 5 to 9) are in bud almost from New Year's Day on. The evergreen leaves are deeply divided; bloom occurs in the plant's second year. Biennial, green-flowered Corsican hellebore (*H. argutifolius*, zones 6 to 9) has spiny-toothed evergreen leaves on bushy plants to 4 ft. tall. Perhaps the best loved is 12-in. tall Christmas rose (*H. niger*, zones 4 to 8). In Europe it is grown under glass for Christmas bouquets. It is a fussy grower, needing shade and moisture-retaining sweet soil.

A drift or mass planting of Lenten roses under oaks or hickory in early spring is a special sight.

Longspur barrenwort

Epimedium grandiflorum

BARRENWORTS or bishop's hats are both tough and delicate-looking, and make stunning specimens or groundcovers. Used medicinally since ancient times, they contain some of the same anthocyanins that related barberry (*Berberis*) contains, ensuring that deer only dine on them when they are desperate for food.

Deciduous longspur barrenwort is native to Japan, North Korea, and parts of Manchuria but is popular in shade and woodland gardens in the United States and Canada. The wiry-stemmed foliage is twice divided into spiny-toothed, 2-in. leaflets. When young these may be attractively rimmed in red; other species have red veining, too. The spidery, 1½-in., reddish flowers, with curved-back, ½-in., white spurs, are borne in loose sprays well above the leaves.

HOW TO GROW

Barrenworts do best in acid, humus-rich soil in lightly shaded woodlands where the soil does not dry out in summer. That said, dry places under the shade of deciduous trees and shrubs can also be colonized. Vigorous longspur epimediums are probably the best suited to these difficult sites. Carve out the soil from between a couple of big main roots and replace it with really good, humus-rich soil that retains moisture. Plant carefully and apply organic mulch each season.

After bloom time, the foliage remains handsome until cold weather; fall color is unreliable, but the leaves hang on. Leave the tan-colored dead foliage through the winter and cut it back just as new growth starts in spring. In mild climates longspur barrenwort remains evergreen. Divide clumps after bloom time or during the growing season.

QUICK LOOK

Hardiness
Zones 4–8
Height and spread
8–15 in. × 15 in.
Deer resistance rating
9–10

DESIGN TIPS

Barrenworts are great massed in light woodlands, but
some species bulk up readily and others make better specimen plants. Longspur barrenwort is a vigorous clumping
plant; plant several together to develop large patches. Any
of its cultivars, including 'Rose Queen' with deep rose
flowers sometimes having white-tipped spurs, all-white
'White Queen', and 'Lilafee' with lavender-violet flowers,
can be used elegantly under shrubs or along the base of
hedges. In woodlands, mix with mayapple (*Podophyllum
peltatum*), assorted ferns, white wood aster (*Aster divaricatus*), and Canadian wild ginger (*Asarum canadense*). Other
good groundcover species include yellow *Epimedium
pinnatum* subsp. *colchicum* and red-flowered *E. ×rubrum*. In
shaded rock gardens, clumping, white-flowered Young's
epimedium (*E. ×youngianum*) is perfect. Growing 6 to 8 in.
tall, its heart-shaped, medium green leaves are on wiry
reddish stems. Plant Young's epimedium along walkways
or paths to bloom after snowdrops (*Galanthus*), Siberian
squills (*Scilla sibirica*), or grape hyacinths (*Muscari*). Other
companions could include yellow ferny corydalis (*Corydalis cheilanthifolia*), yellow daisy-flowered green-and-gold
(*Chrysogonum virginianum*), and blue columbine (*Aquilegia
bertolonii*). White-flowered 'Niveum' and pink 'Roseum'
are both charming, perhaps paired with crested iris (*Iris
cristata*) and mountain lady's mantle (*Alchemilla alpina*).
They also adapt well to crevice gardens and between
patio pavers, maybe accompanied by mother-of-thyme
(*Thymus serpyllum*).

Any of its cultivars
can be used elegantly
under shrubs or along
the base of hedges.

White longspur barrenwort (*Epimedium grandiflorum* 'Album').

97

Peony

Paeonia officinalis

ROMANTIC PEONIES seem to speak of another time, when long-skirted ladies snipped flowers for the house. Many of the same individuals planted almost one hundred years ago still bloom. These plants are very tough and easy to grow when given full sun and good soil. Pests and diseases are few, and deer, unimpressed with their strong scent, seldom browse them except for a bloom or two. Many species, in particular Asian *Paeonia lactiflora*, have been involved in their evolution. Named cultivars abound in all colors except blue, and with various heights, bloom times, flower shapes, and sizes. Consult the American Peony Society (americanpeonysociety.org) for detailed information.

Peony bloom time begins in early May in most zones and continues through the month. In the South it is earlier, and wise southern gardeners select early or midseason varieties to bloom prior to the onset of hot weather.

HOW TO GROW

Peonies are very greedy and need lots of moisture-retaining organic material to do their best. Select a site with full sun and well-drained, rich, fertile soil. Plant the crowns 2 to 3 ft. apart and no more than 2 in. below the soil surface; deep planting inhibits blooming as much as does lack of sun. Add compost, well-rotted manure, or decomposed leaves to the soil at planting time and water deeply. Plant bare-root peonies in fall (they are seldom available at other times), but containerized plants can be planted in spring or fall. It may take two or three seasons before they bloom freely. Ants are attracted to the sweet nectar on the flower buds; they are harmless, but wash them off before arranging cut flowers indoors.

QUICK LOOK

Hardiness
Zones 3–8
Height and spread
1½–3½ ft. × 2–3 ft.
Deer resistance rating
7–10

'Don Richardson' peony (*Paeonia* 'Don Richardson').

Many of the same individuals planted almost one hundred years ago still bloom.

DESIGN TIPS

After blooming, the dark, twice-divided foliage of garden peonies remains handsome until frost and often displays fall color; lobed seedpods split open to reveal red or black seeds. These attributes make garden peonies attractive in three seasons and an excellent choice in sunny beds and borders combined with perennials, bulbs, annuals, or shrubs. In mixed borders plant peonies with later-blooming silvery bluebeard (*Caryopteris*) and Russian sage (*Perovskia*). Evergreen Japanese andromeda (*Pieris*) and Armstrong juniper (*Juniperus chinensis* 'Armstrongii') make nice backdrops. Fragrant mock orange (*Philadelphus*), bush cinquefoil (*Potentilla fruticosa*), and Japanese flowering quince (*Chaenomeles*) are also attractive flowering shrub companions. Hardy geraniums such as 'Rozanne' or a bloody cranesbill (*Geranium sanguineum*) cultivar in a compatible color play off well against peonies. Gaura, speedwells (*Veronica*), mulleins (*Verbascum*), and sages (*Salvia*) are also good players. In cottage gardens, lavender (*Lavandula*), German iris (*Iris* ×*germanica*), and rosemary (*Rosmarinus officinalis*) create a pleasing scene, perhaps planted under tall, out-of-reach lilac (*Syringa*). Since peony plants are visually dense, a single specimen suffices in limited space, but if possible group several plants with different forms, colors, and bloom times. Flowers come single, double, semidouble, and in Japanese forms according to the number of petals. Some popular cultivars include midseason, double, pale pink 'Angel Cheeks'; early, single, white 'Krinkled White'; early, semidouble, dark coral 'Coral Charm'; early to midseason Japanese-type, deep red 'Don Richardson'; and midseason, Japanese-type, cherry red and pink 'Gay Paree'. Peonies are excellent as cut flowers; in the trade many come from New Zealand for our Thanksgiving market. Cut them when the flowers are still in soft bud, and condition them overnight in cool water.

Siberian bugloss

Brunnera macrophylla

A S ITS COMMON NAME implies, tough and hardy Siberian bugloss (also known as heart-leaved brunnera, perennial forget-me-not, and false forget-me-not) hails from frigid winter regions in eastern Europe and Siberia. It is a perfect candidate for gardens exposed to cold winters in parts of the United States and Canada. This low-maintenance, adaptable perennial, sometimes found under the name *Anchusa myosotidiflora*, remains attractive even after the airy sprays of yellow-eyed, blue forget-me-not flowers fade by early summer. Then the lightly hairy, somewhat coarse, broadly heart-shaped, emerald leaves expand to 6 to 8 in. wide and continue to grace the garden all summer. Their rough texture is seldom palatable to deer.

HOW TO GROW

Siberian bugloss thrives in light or dappled shade in most soils as long as they remain moist. Improve drainage and moisture retention at planting time with applications of organic material such as compost or rotted bark chips. An organic mulch in summer reduces surface moisture evaporation. Drying out results in crisping of the leaf edges, as does too much sun; white- and cream-variegated cultivars are particularly prone to sunburn. Clip spent flowers to the crown after bloom time along with shabby leaves if necessary. Except to increase stock, division is only necessary when the centers of the plants deteriorate, probably after four or five years. Do this in early spring. Root cuttings can also be taken in early spring, but variegated selections seldom retain their variegation and are best propagated by division. Late-summer and fall sowings of seeds reach bloom size in one to two years.

QUICK LOOK

Hardiness
Zones 3–8
Height and spread
1–1½ ft. × 1½–2 ft.
Deer resistance rating
8–9

DESIGN TIPS

Planted 1 to 1½ ft. apart, Siberian buglosses make a fine groundcover among shrubs. Their abundant basal leaves cover the ground, shading out weeds and cutting down on maintenance. They thrive alongside lightly shaded streams and ponds, perhaps with later-blooming Japanese iris (*Iris ensata*) and sedges, developing into healthy colonies in a short time.

When flowers are past, this plant's value in beds and borders turns to the foliage, which remains handsome. The variegated cultivars, mostly with pale blue flowers, are particularly popular. 'Variegata' and 'Dawson's White' (possibly synonyms) sport wide cream margins that are susceptible to burning. They are especially attractive grouped with dark-leaved shrubs and evergreens such as *Weigela* Midnight Wine ('Elvera') and Siberian cypress (*Microbiota decussata*). Single specimens stand out in large rock gardens; avoid planting them where they will overcome alpine gems. An appropriate cultivar is 'Emerald Mist' with irregular patches of silver encircling an emerald heart within a green margin. The British introduction 'Langtrees' (also known as 'Aluminum Spot') displays delicate silver "ditto" marks along its leaf edges, a perfect echo for 'White Nancy' deadnettle (*Lamium maculatum* 'White Nancy'). Silver-leaved 'Jack Frost' is heavily veined and rimmed with emerald, and glowing 'Looking Glass' is almost all silver with just a slender emerald edge. In a woodland garden, both are striking partners for bright yellow celandine poppy (*Stylophorum diphyllum*), low ferns, and later-blooming white or pastel astilbes. Also look for 'Spring Yellow', whose young foliage emerges butter yellow in dramatic contrast with sky blue flowers. 'Diane's Gold' is said to retain its chartreuse leaf color all summer.

Silver-leaved 'Jack Frost' is heavily veined and rimmed with emerald, and glowing 'Looking Glass' is almost all silver with just a slender emerald edge.

Variegated Siberian bugloss (*Brunnera macrophylla* 'Variegata').

Yarrow

Achillea millefolium

'Terracotta' yarrow (*Achillea millefolium* 'Terracotta').

ACHILLEA MILLEFOLIUM is abundant in many parts of its native Europe, where it is considered invasive, and is widely naturalized across North America along roadsides and waste places. However, it has given rise to numerous beautiful, garden-worthy cultivars and hybrids with butterfly-attracting flowers in shades of pink, crimson, lilac, orange, yellow, and red. These make fine, well-behaved garden plants for sunny or lightly shaded gardens, although they tend to spread by creeping rhizomes and need division every few years. Deer find the slightly acrid aromatic foliage distasteful and avoid browsing it.

HOW TO GROW

Yarrows do best where soil is lean to poor, with good drainage. They tolerate dry conditions well and are suitable for xeric gardens. Overly rich or fertile soil produces less aromatic, soft growth that will need staking. Deadhead spent flower heads to lateral buds after bloom time to encourage further flowers.

DESIGN TIPS

Sunny perennial and mixed borders are ideal spots for yarrows. With such a wide range of colors, it is not difficult to create fun combinations. Try using 1½-ft. 'Summer Pastels' (it blooms its first summer) with 'May Night' hybrid sage (*Salvia* ×*sylvestris* 'May Night'), 'Siskiyou Pink' gaura (*Gaura lindheimeri* 'Siskiyou Pink'), *Veronica* 'Sunny Border Blue', or 'Moonbeam' threadleaf coreopsis (*Coreopsis verticillata* 'Moonbeam'). These also work well with 'Terracotta', a yellow-centered, reddish-salmon-flowered, 1- to 2-ft. cultivar that changes color as it matures; deadhead for many weeks of bloom. In the rosy pink range,

Compact habit is a trait of the Seduction series, all less than 2 ft. tall, in real red ('Strawberry Seduction'), rosy pink ('Saucy Seduction'), and butter yellow ('Sunny Seduction').

'Appleblossom' has been largely replaced by 2½-ft. tall 'Oertel's Rose', especially in the South. The flowers mature almost to white. Purplish ornamental oregano (*Origanum laevigatum* 'Herrenhausen') is a particularly attractive companion. Soft russet 'Sawa Sawa' fades to light yellow. Its strong 2½-ft. stems make it superior as a cut flower. Compact habit is a trait of the Seduction series, all less than 2 ft. tall, in real red ('Strawberry Seduction'), rosy pink ('Saucy Seduction'), and butter yellow ('Sunny Seduction'). The latter two have silvery leaves. In butterfly and wildlife gardens, plant yarrows with pincushion flower (*Scabiosa* 'Butterfly Blue' or 'Pink Mist'), shrub verbena (*Lantana camara*), and purple coneflower (*Echinacea*). They attract not only butterflies but also hoverflies and a host of other insects. From the Caucasus Mountains, clumping fern-leaf yarrow (*Achillea filipendulina*) has feathery gray-green foliage and flattened heads of bright yellow flowers on leafy stems. Reliable cultivars include 5-ft. tall, deep yellow 'Gold Plate', somewhat shorter 'Cloth of Gold', and more golden 'Parker's Variety'. Fern-leaf yarrows are handsome among Russian sage (*Perovskia*) and bluebeard (*Caryopteris*). Hybrids 'Coronation Gold' with brilliant gold, 4-in. flower heads atop strong, leafy, 2- to 4-ft. stems, and lemon yellow, 1- to 2-ft. 'Moonshine' also have silvery leaves. At less than 12 in. tall, yellow woolly yarrow (*A. tomentosa*) is suitable for rock gardens and crevices, but only in cool zones—it melts in hot, humid climates. All of these yarrows also make long-lasting fresh-cut or dried flowers.

Shrubs

Russian cypress (*Microbiota decussata*) softens the
wall in front of white-blooming deutzia, with ferns
behind.

Bluebeard

Caryopteris ×clandonensis

WITH SILVERY, aromatic leaves and clusters of fluffy blue flowers in late summer, bluebeard is a valuable addition to sunny sites at a time when color is often scarce. The flowers, with their exserted stamens, give the effect of a fine mist of blue, hence another name: blue mistflower. A chance hybrid, bluebeard was originally found in an English garden. It is a tough, fine-textured shrub that blooms on new wood and attracts butterflies during its extended bloom time. Deer do not appreciate the aroma of the leaves.

HOW TO GROW

Plant bluebeard in a sunny spot in well-drained and fertile but not overly rich soil. When established the plants tolerate some drought, but apply a summer mulch to retain soil moisture. Pests and diseases are seldom a problem. Set plants 4 to 5 ft. apart and avoid planting too deeply. Low branches often layer themselves, adding to the girth of the plant. Detach these young layered plants or propagate by rooting softwood cuttings in summer. Prune hard in spring when at least ½ in. of new growth has sprouted. In northern climates, treat bluebeard as an herbaceous perennial; new shoots break from the base.

DESIGN TIPS

Several first-rate cultivars are available. 'Longwood Blue' is a 4-ft. tall favorite with bluish purple flowers. 'Azure' and 'Blue Mist' have pale blue flowers. At 2 ft. tall, dark purple 'First Choice' is ideal for small gardens. In spring 'Worcester Gold' produces yellow foliage that unfortunately greens up as summer progresses. Yellow-foliaged

QUICK LOOK

Hardiness
Zones 6–9
Height and spread
3–4 ft. × 3–5 ft.
Deer resistance rating
9–10

Bluebeard (*Caryopteris ×clandonensis* 'Longwood Blue') with *Rudbeckia fulgida* 'Goldsturm'.

Caryopteris incana Sunshine Blue ('Jason') holds its leaf color better, with rich blue flowers.

Bluebeard fits well in many parts of the garden. With shrubs, use it in the foreground or middle of the border, perhaps with dark-leaved *Weigela florida* Wine and Roses ('Alexandra') behind. Evergreen boxwood (*Buxus*) or dense 'Rose Creek' glossy abelia (*Abelia ×grandiflora* 'Rose Creek') would provide a solid contrast to airy bluebeard. Shrubby bush cinquefoils (*Potentilla fruticosa*) 'Apricot Whisper', 'Pink Beauty', and bright yellow Dakota Sunspot ('Fargo') are other good choices. In deer-resistant mixed beds and borders the selection of plants to accompany bluebeard is only limited by culture preferences and your own color choices. Blanket flowers (*Gaillardia* 'Oranges and Lemons' is excellent) and purple coneflowers (*Echinacea* cultivars such as pink 'Merlot', rosy purple 'Magnus', orange 'Art's Pride', yellow 'Sunrise', and white 'Milkshake' or 'White Lustre') come to mind, providing daisy shapes that contrast well with the bloom, foliage color, and habit of bluebeard. For containers, compact, 2-ft. tall 'Petit Bleu' is superior to other cultivars, with good branching and abundant flowers. Soften the edges of the planter with trailing golden creeping Jenny (*Lysimachia nummularia* 'Aurea') or *Sedum* 'Angelina'. 'Golden Baby' goldenrod (*Solidago* 'Golden Baby'), *Agastache* 'Apricot Sunrise', 'Moonbeam' threadleaf coreopsis (*Coreopsis verticillata* 'Moonbeam'), and 'Siskiyou Pink' gaura (*Gaura lindheimeri* 'Siskiyou Pink') are appropriate companions in planters or in the ground. Elsewhere plant 4-ft. tall, very deep blue 'Dark Knight' or 'Heavenly Blue' in front of stone walls or beside formal steps. Bluebeard also works well as an informal hedge or low misty screen, especially with ornamental grasses.

The flowers, with their exserted stamens, give the effect of a fine mist of blue, hence another name: blue mistflower.

Boxwood

Buxus species and cultivars

OXWOODS are the signature plants of formal gardens, usually clipped into hedges, balls, or other topiary forms. They have been grown since Roman times and were once widely cultivated for their very hard wood, which carves well. Though popular in Colonial and knot gardens, as at Colonial Williamsburg, boxwoods are now often grown without routine clipping, reflecting the less formal style of many contemporary gardens. Plenty of boxwoods are on the market, mostly cultivars or hybrids derived from common or American boxwood (*Buxus sempervirens*, 5 to 10 ft. tall) and heat-tolerant Japanese boxwood (*B. microphylla*, 2 to 3 ft. tall). Both species have small, dark green, evergreen leaves; those of common boxwood are yellow beneath, while Japanese boxwood's leaves are brighter green. They have a strong odor that deer dislike.

HOW TO GROW

Boxwoods do best in semishaded spots where the soil drains freely. They do not tolerate wet feet and should be planted with the top of the root ball just at soil level. Water them deeply and keep moist until established. Shallow, wide-spreading roots benefit from the addition of 2 to 3 in. of organic mulch to retain moisture and keep the soil cool. In winter, wrap large shrubs with strong cord to prevent snow forcing open the interior; in cold regions homeowners protect boxwoods with burlap or screening to reduce winter wind damage. Winter drought, sunburn, and cold cause reddish brown or discolored leaves and sometimes branch dieback. Damaged growth can be cut out in spring. Be alert for pests such as leaf miner and

QUICK LOOK

Hardiness
Zones 4–9
Height and spread
2–10 ft. × 3 ft. or more
Deer resistance rating
9–10

psyllids, and treat accordingly. Propagate from summer cuttings.

DESIGN TIPS

Boxwoods come in many different forms, and particular habits should be selected for specific purposes. For example, 2- to 3-ft. tall 'Vardar Valley' (zones 5 to 8) is a good choice for foundation plantings. In warm climates, variegated 'Elegantissima' (zones 6 to 8) looks well as a specimen plant in beds among coral bells (*Heuchera*) and other low foliage perennials. As a hedge, try dense 'Green Velvet' (zones 5 to 9) or 'Wintergreen', a hardy, compact grower well adapted to warmer climates. In the North, hybrid cultivars such as 'Green Gem', upright 'Green Mountain', and 'Northern Charm' (zones 4 to 8) are recommended.

In shrub or mixed borders, use boxwoods as evergreen accents at the front of the border, perhaps combined with weeping cutleaf stephanandra (*Stephanandra incisa* 'Crispa') or low-growing Japanese skimmia (*Skimmia japonica*). For a strong contrast in form and color, add variegated Hakone grass (*Hakonechloa macra* 'Aureola'). Use large boxwoods such as slender, upright 'Graham Blandy' as a vertical accent or at the rear of the border, perhaps with a bold ornamental grass for a great winter contrast. As a specimen it could be a living support for a white perennial pea (*Lathyrus latifolius* 'Alba'). Traditionally so-called English boxwood (*Buxus sempervirens* 'Suffruticosa', zones 6 to 8) has been the plant of choice for formal, low, clipped hedges. This dense, slow-growing plant may reach 5 ft. eventually if left unclipped. However, it is very amenable to clipping and can easily be kept at several inches tall, perfect for edgings and borders.

Boxwoods are now often grown without routine clipping, reflecting the less formal style of many contemporary gardens.

Formally clipped boxwood (*Buxus* hybrid).

Bush cinquefoil

Potentilla fruticosa

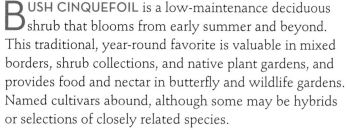

QUICK LOOK

Hardiness
Zones 2–7
Height and spread
2–5 ft. × 3–5 ft.
Deer resistance rating
9–10

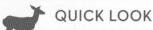

'Goldfinger' bush cinquefoil (*Potentilla fruticosa* 'Goldfinger').

BUSH CINQUEFOIL is a low-maintenance deciduous shrub that blooms from early summer and beyond. This traditional, year-round favorite is valuable in mixed borders, shrub collections, and native plant gardens, and provides food and nectar in butterfly and wildlife gardens. Named cultivars abound, although some may be hybrids or selections of closely related species.

This slow-growing, bushy shrub is native to north temperate regions, including North America. Broadly rounded with upright stems, it is attractive in winter for both its shape and brown bark, which peels with age. The ¾- to 1-in. flowers are saucer-shaped and, in the species, bright yellow, either carried singly or a few together. The first flush of bloom covers the bushes in early to midsummer, with more flowers coming until fall. Foliage is fine-textured, silky gray-green in early spring, usually becoming green as it matures. The pinnate leaves have five or seven slender leaflets, each about an inch long. Deer do not find the hairy leaves appetizing.

HOW TO GROW
Plant bush cinquefoil in full sun or in a partly shaded spot where the soil is fertile and retains moisture yet drains well. Too much shade or poor soil usually reduces the amount of bloom. Amend the soil with plenty of organic material at planting time, and mulch in summer, especially in full sun. Although bush cinquefoil tolerates warm temperatures, it does not enjoy high humidity or high night temperatures. It does best in midwestern and northern gardens, not so well in the South. Blooms appear on new growth. Prune in late winter to remove old canes. Severe pruning is recommended every few years.

The first flush of bloom covers the bushes in early to midsummer, with more flowers coming until fall.

DESIGN TIPS

Bush cinquefoil is a real workhorse for its ease of culture and long bloom time. Among the best cultivars, several stand out. Try 18-in. tall Canadian 'Lemon Gem' at the front of the border, in containers, as a low groundcover, or as a hedge. It may reach 2 ft. across with grayish leaves and bright yellow, somewhat ruffled flowers. Similar in size, 'Sunset' has yellow flowers tinged with reddish orange. Catmint (*Nepeta*) and upright speedwells (*Veronica*) are attractive partners. One of the best whites is 'Abbotswood', which at 3 ft. tall is ideal for the midsection of a border. Creamy white 'McKay's White' is somewhat shorter. Variegated snow-on-the-mountain (*Euphorbia marginata*), 'Paprika' yarrow (*Achillea* 'Paprika'), and blue angelonia (*Angelonia angustifolia*) make colorful companions. Superior yellow cultivars include 3-ft. tall profuse bloomer 'Gold Drop' ('Farreri'), low 'Goldstar' with 2-in. flowers, and large-flowered 'Goldfinger'. Combine with Russian sage (*Perovskia*) and bluebeard (*Caryopteris*) for color contrast in late summer. Abundant bright yellow flowers grace long-blooming, 4-ft. tall 'Coronation Triumph', which is especially successful in cold regions of the United States and Canada. It is excellent as an informal hedge, perhaps behind blue oat grass (*Helictotrichon sempervirens*) or 'Heavy Metal' blue switch grass (*Panicum virgatum* 'Heavy Metal'). Popular 'Primrose Beauty' blooms for several months with large, pale creamy yellow flowers. Pink-flowered cultivars tend to fade in the South but are excellent in cool-summer regions where sun is less intense. Mounding 'Pink Pearl' has midpink blooms with yellow undertones. Clear pink 'Pink Beauty' fades to very pale pink or white where nights are warm.

Cutleaf stephanandra

Stephanandra incisa 'Crispa'

CUTLEAF STEPHANANDRA is another great plant from eastern Asia, where it grows wild at the edges of woodlands, forming dense thickets. The species, also known as *Neillia incisa* (you'll find it in catalogs and nurseries under either name), is seldom seen in cultivation, but the compact 'Crispa' is readily available. This fine-textured shrub is suitable for gardens where space is limited, although it can spread to several feet across. Its arching, zigzagging stems, clothed with cinnamon-colored bark in winter, bear triangular, lobed and toothed, bright green leaves alternately along their length. In late spring, 3-in. long clusters of small, greenish white, starry flowers bloom on young growth and are quite pretty. The supple stems grow quickly and form a mounding tangle. In fall the foliage turns dusty orange before it drops, leaving a thicket of woody stems for the winter. Deer must be afraid to get their feet tangled in the plant and avoid browsing it.

HOW TO GROW

Plant 'Crispa' in full sun or part shade in moisture-retaining, humus-rich soil that drains well. Slightly acid soil is ideal, but cutleaf stephanandra is not that fussy. Stems often root where they touch the ground, increasing the girth of the plant; detach these young plantlets to increase stock, or take softwood cuttings in early summer. Prune back too-long stems after bloom if necessary, and cut out old woody growth to the ground. 'Crispa' remains pest and disease free and requires little maintenance.

QUICK LOOK

Hardiness
Zones 4–8
Height and spread
1–3 ft. × 2–4 ft.
Deer resistance rating
9–10

DESIGN TIPS

In the garden make good use of the cat's cradle of branch-es that 'Crispa' develops. Plant it to cover awkward banks that are difficult to mow, where it helps to control soil erosion. Allow it to tumble over low walls and masonry, or use it as a tall groundcover. I have seen it used to good effect as a hedgelike groundcover beside steep steps. As an informal hedge, 'Crispa' takes clipping well, but only really needs it once a year or so. At the front of shrub col-lections, allow it to soften the edge of the border, perhaps with 'Nikko' slender deutzia (*Deutzia gracilis* 'Nikko'), low, evergreen Russian cypress (*Microbiota decussata*), or round-ed Japanese skimmia (*Skimmia japonica*). Taller shrubs, including dark-leaved *Weigela florida* Wine and Roses ('Alexandra') and later-to-bloom rose of Sharon (*Hibiscus syriacus*), would be interesting behind. In mixed borders, contrast 'Crispa' with taller perennials, grasses, and shrubs. For summer, try purple coneflower (*Echinacea*), butterfly weed (*Asclepias tuberosa*), tall meadow rues (*Thal-ictrum*), and catmint (*Nepeta*) behind. Annuals work well, too—spider flower (*Cleome*), flowering tobacco (*Nicotiana*), and larkspur (*Consolida ajacis*) provide colorful backdrops for much of spring and summer. Tall ornamental onions (*Allium*) make a splash in the border, but dying foliage at the base is unsightly. Plant a large group of maroon drumstick allium (*A. sphaerocephalon*) among and around 'Crispa'; the bulbs will grow through and be supported by the stems, which will also hide the dying foliage. Also try letting annual nasturtiums (*Tropaeolum majus*) scramble over a thicket of 'Crispa' stems.

The supple stems grow quickly and form a mounding tangle. In fall the foliage turns dusty orange before it drops, leaving a thicket of woody stems for the winter.

Cutleaf stephanandra (*Stephanandra incisa* 'Crispa').

English lavender

Lavandula angustifolia

NATIVE TO the Mediterranean region, English lavender has been a staple herb for centuries, beloved for its compact spikes of lavender-blue flowers, aromatic gray-green leaves, and uniquely fragrant, deer-unfriendly essential oils. It is used as an antiseptic, relaxant, and remedy for burns, depression, and other complaints, and its economic value to the perfumery and toiletries industry is untold. Most lavender grown for essential oils is farmed in eastern England, southern France, Tasmania, and New Zealand. Other, more tender species and hybrids of note include French lavender (*Lavandula stoechas*, zones 8 to 9), Spanish lavender or rabbit ears (*L. stoechas* subsp. *pedunculata*, zones 8 to 11), fringed lavender (*L. dentata*, zones 8 to 11), and the so-called lavandins (English lavender crossed with spike lavender, zones 7 to 11).

HOW TO GROW

Mediterranean soils tend to be slightly alkaline, stony, very well drained, and rather poor. These are ideal conditions for growing lavender, although average garden soil is fine if it drains freely; root rot results from poor drainage and too rich a soil. Select a sunny site for lavender so that the essential oils become concentrated. Space plants about 2 ft. apart (closer for hedging) and incorporate some gritty material (turkey grit is good) at the base if drainage might be a problem. Keep young plants watered; once established, they tolerate drought well. Prune back to about 6 to 8 in. in spring only after new growth appears; hard pruning too early, especially in chilly climates, is often fatal. Harvest flowers for drying when they show color.

QUICK LOOK

Hardiness
Zones 6–9
Height and spread
1–4 ft. × 2–4 ft.
Deer resistance rating
9–10

English lavender (*Lavandula angustifolia*).

Lavender is a traditional component in cottage and dooryard gardens, where it can be kept close at hand for flavoring in the kitchen (try lavender scones) and for first aid.

DESIGN TIPS

Shrubby English lavender is an elegant addition to many parts of the garden where cultural conditions allow. For rock gardens or containers, select compact forms (1-ft. tall 'Munstead', 'Silver Frost', or white-flowered 'Nana Alba'). Hedges of lavender (*Lavandula angustifolia* 'Hidcote' is a good selection) can be beautiful if grown well and not allowed to get leggy. Set out young plants 6 to 9 in. apart, ideally on top of a bank or raised bed to ensure excellent drainage. After bloom, trim the top and sides back to strong shoots to force attractive bushy growth. Traditionally lavender has been grown as a companion for roses, but this may not work in deer country. West Coast vineyards grow hedges of lavender to enhance the tourist experience, and the lavender fields of Provence are a popular tourist destination (check out the Abbey Notre-Dame de Sénanque near Gordes).

Other silver-leaved shrubs thrive in similar conditions and combine well, including Thunberg bush clover (*Lespedeza thunbergii*) and Russian sage (*Perovskia*). Accompany them with colorful annuals like floss flower (*Ageratum houstonianum*), spider flower (*Cleome*), strawflower (*Helichrysum*), and poppies. Tickseeds (*Coreopsis*), Stokes' aster (*Stokesia*), lamb's ears (*Stachys byzantina*), and other perennials are also suitable companions. Lavender is a traditional component in cottage and dooryard gardens, where it can be kept close at hand for flavoring in the kitchen (try lavender scones) and for first aid. In herb gardens, lavender is a natural partner for culinary herbs and horehound (*Marrubium*), scented geraniums (*Pelargonium*), hummingbird mints (*Agastache*), ornamental onions (*Allium*), and catmints (*Nepeta*).

Japanese spirea

Spiraea japonica

THIS SPECIES has made itself quite at home in North America, reaching the point of invasiveness in the eastern United States, Ontario, and Nova Scotia, where it seeds abundantly and develops into large stands, especially on disturbed land, outcompeting native species and changing the ecology of the area. Luckily, a host of better-behaved cultivars, hybrids, and other selections are available to grace our gardens in style. Other superior spireas include 'Snowmound' Nippon spirea (*Spiraea nipponica* 'Snowmound'), bridal wreath (*S. prunifolia*), and Van Houtte spirea (*S. ×vanhouttei*). It is not clear why deer seldom browse spireas, but countless reports confirm that deer find them unpalatable.

Immensely variable, Japanese spireas develop into stands of dense, mounding shrubs with lots of twiggy growth. The small leaves, often serrated along the margins, vary in color by cultivar from blue-green and green to yellow. The flattish flower clusters, composed of countless, usually pink, ¼-in. flowers, bloom in summer, mostly on new wood.

HOW TO GROW

Shear off spent flower clusters after bloom time to avoid seeding and to encourage a later crop. Japanese spirea can be treated as an herbaceous perennial and pruned hard in early spring. It thrives in sunny or very lightly shaded spots in fertile, well-drained soil. Depending upon the ultimate size, space shrubs 2 to 4 ft. apart or wider. Propagate by rooting softwood cuttings in summer. Few pests and diseases are a problem, although aphids may attack young growth.

QUICK LOOK

Hardiness
Zones 4–8
Height and spread
1–6 ft. × 2–6 ft.
Deer resistance rating
9–10

DESIGN TIPS

Japanese spirea cultivars are suitable for many parts of the garden. For rock gardens, select 1- to 2-ft. tall 'Alpina', also known as daphne spirea. Its light pink flowers appear in early summer and combine well with late pink daffodils, pinks (*Dianthus*), and pastel Shirley poppies (*Papaver rhoeas*). Or plant it close as a groundcover, perhaps along a path or walkway. Pale pink, 2½-ft. tall 'Little Princess' is better suited to mixed borders. It shines with pink peonies (such as *Paeonia lactiflora* 'Monsieur Jules Elie') and oriental poppies (*Papaver orientale* 'Cedric Morris'). 'Anthony Waterer', often considered under *Spiraea ×bumalda*, varies according to clone, both in terms of size (to 6 ft. tall) and flower color (ideally deep carmine red). The bronzy young foliage greens up later. This useful filler for the shrub border also makes a fine hedge. Green-foliaged 'Neon Flash' makes a splash with its bright red flower clusters. It grows fast to about 3 ft. tall and wide. In fall the leaves turn burgundy. Golden-leaved, 2-ft. tall Double Play Gold ('Yan') can be used for low hedges, as a specimen, or grouped at the front of shrub collections. The leaves retain their golden color through the season, unlike those of 'Golden Princess', which often fade. 'Goldflame' turns coppery in fall. If pink flowers over yellow leaves are not to your taste, 3-ft. tall 'White Gold' might appeal; its white flower clusters bloom above bright golden foliage that holds its color well, though the plant may need protection from intense sun. All of these appealingly easy-care varieties have a place in butterfly and cottage gardens.

Green-foliaged 'Neon Flash' makes a splash with its bright red flower clusters.

An informal hedge of Japanese spirea (*Spiraea japonica*).

127

Purple beautyberry

Callicarpa dichotoma

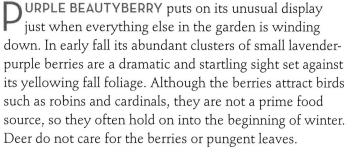

PURPLE BEAUTYBERRY puts on its unusual display just when everything else in the garden is winding down. In early fall its abundant clusters of small lavender-purple berries are a dramatic and startling sight set against its yellowing fall foliage. Although the berries attract birds such as robins and cardinals, they are not a prime food source, so they often hold on into the beginning of winter. Deer do not care for the berries or pungent leaves.

Native to China and Japan, purple beautyberry is a rapid-growing deciduous shrub with an arching habit. Medium green leaves are borne along each side of the stems in a single plane. Clusters of small pink flowers bloom in summer on new wood.

HOW TO GROW

Purple beautyberry does best in full sun or light shade with well-drained but not overly rich soil. Adequate soil moisture is important, but established plants tolerate drought well. Group several together, roughly 5 ft. apart, to effect cross-pollination for the best berry production, although this species is mostly self-fertile. In cold climates treat beautyberry as an herbaceous perennial; prune it hard in early spring, and young growth will break from the base.

DESIGN TIPS

Callicarpa dichotoma is considered by many to be the best species of beautyberry for fruit production. Forma *albifructa* is slightly taller with white berries. 'Issai' produces fruit on young plants before they mature, offering instant gratification for gardeners. A variegated form, 'Splashy', has the same purple berries as the species, but its foliage

QUICK LOOK

Hardiness
Zones 5–8
Height and spread
3–4 ft. × 3–5 ft.
Deer resistance rating
8–10

Purple beautyberry (*Callicarpa dichotoma*) in fruit.

In early fall its abundant clusters of small lavender-purple berries are a dramatic and startling sight set against its yellowing fall foliage.

is irregularly splashed and streaked with white. Among other cultivars on the market, 'Early Amethyst' is the first to produce berries, which sometimes appear in August. In zones 8 to 10, try *Callicarpa acuminata* 'Woodlanders', reported to have extremely dark berries. 'Profusion', a cultivar of Bodinier's beautyberry (*C. bodinieri* var. *giraldii*), grows about 6 to 8 ft. tall with large clusters of bright berries; it does best in zones 6 to 8.

Native-plant aficionados favor American beautyberry (*Callicarpa americana*), native to the Southeast. Where it is hardy (zones 7 to 10), it is a great choice for shrub collections in native plant and wild gardens, as well as for hedges. Its profuse clusters of bright purple berries (white in *C. americana* var. *lactea* and its cultivar 'Bok Tower') follow light pink summer flowers. Foliage is large, hairy, and rough.

In shrub borders try purple beautyberry against a backdrop of evergreens such as Japanese andromeda (*Pieris*), American holly (*Ilex americana*), or even creeping juniper (*Juniperus horizontalis*). Since their season of impact is limited, a mixture of other shrubs that peak during other times is appropriate. Consider Japanese flowering quince (*Chaenomeles japonica*), weigelas, and Carolina silverbells (*Halesia carolina*) for spring, and summersweet (*Clethra*) and bluebeard (*Caryopteris*) for later color. Late-blooming colchicums massed in a pool beneath purple beautyberry produce a dramatic effect. *Miscanthus*, pampas grass (*Cortaderia selloana*), and other large ornamental grasses provide interesting backdrops in fall, while lower growers such as fountain grasses (*Pennisetum*) and switch grasses (*Panicum*) make good contrasting companions.

Russian cypress

Microbiota decussata

I F YOU ARE looking for a tough, slow-growing, ever-green groundcover, Russian cypress will serve well. Also known as Siberian carpet, this plant is native to cold regions of eastern Russia, but it adapts well to cooler regions of the United States and Canada. A dense, low-growing, flat-topped conifer, it looks from a distance like a juniper, but closer inspection reveals that the flattened, triangular sprays of scalelike foliage are feathery and lacy, drooping at the tips. In early spring the foliage becomes bright green, turning darker as the season progresses; it takes on a purplish cast when cold weather arrives. Plants are unisexual, with males and females on different plants (monoecious); scaly fruits are borne on female plants. The slender stems are clothed with reddish bark that is barely visible unless the foliage is moved aside. Deer have never browsed this plant in my garden; they apparently do not like the texture of the foliage or the rough, scaly bark.

HOW TO GROW

Russian cypress is easy to grow where drainage is good. It is not fussy about soil and thrives in full sun as well as light shade. In too deep shade, the foliage browns and drops, but with a couple of hours of sunlight it is fine. Space plants about 5 ft. apart in well-drained soil; they fill in quite quickly. Except to control their far-reaching spread, pruning is not necessary, but they tolerate shortening back of the stems without trouble. Russian cypress seems free of pests and diseases. Summer cuttings root well, and it is easy to build stock for an extensive planting.

QUICK LOOK

Hardiness
Zones 3–7
Height and spread
1–3 ft. × 3–5 ft.
Deer resistance rating
9–10

DESIGN TIPS

Russian cypress is a wonderful plant for so many parts of the garden. As a low-maintenance groundcover, it is sufficiently lacy and light to support spring bulbs growing through it—early daffodils such as 'February Gold' and 'Tête-à-tête' look charming doing just that. On difficult banks and slopes, use the extensive stems of Russian cypress to reduce erosion, stabilize the ground, and provide natural cover. Although this low evergreen grows too wide for small rock gardens, where there is space it is strikingly attractive in crevices among large rocks. On the level, paths lined with tolerant Russian cypress are easy to keep clipped for a sharp edge. Maintenance otherwise is almost nonexistent. In the foreground of sunny or lightly shaded shrub collections, plant single specimens, perhaps in front of weeping forsythia, 'Nikko' slender deutzia (*Deutzia gracilis* 'Nikko'), or flowering quince (*Chaenomeles speciosa*) for spring, and silver-leaved bluebeard (*Caryopteris*) or Russian sage (*Perovskia*) to provide bloom later. In shadier spots, combine it with dwarf summersweet (*Clethra* 'Sixteen Candles'). Shade-tolerant perennials including Hakone grass (*Hakonechloa macra* 'Aureola'), astilbes, and sweet woodruff (*Galium odoratum*) combine well. Companionable and colorful summer-blooming annuals might include flowering tobacco (*Nicotiana*), ageratum, strawflowers (*Helichrysum*), and verbenas.

For floral work, sprays of Russian cypress work well as a base for wreaths and are easy to manipulate. They are also useful as filler in flower arrangements. Foliage sprays used to decorate outdoor containers for the holiday season remain green for several months.

Foliage sprays used to decorate outdoor containers for the holiday season remain green for several months.

Russian cypress (*Microbiota decussata*) blankets a wall.

Thunberg bush clover

Lespedeza thunbergii

DURING THAT LULL between summer and early fall, flowers are scarce in many gardens, so the gracefully arching stems of Thunberg bush clover, laden with racemes of small, pink or white, sometimes bicolored, pea flowers, are especially valuable. Native to Japan and China, this deciduous shrub often behaves like an herbaceous perennial in zone 7 and colder; new growth breaks from the base come spring. The spent stems retain an elegant, interesting architecture through the winter. Glistening young shoots bear silvery-haired trifoliate leaves and grow rapidly to several feet. The flowers bend the branches toward the ground, creating a colorful fountain effect. The seeds that follow may be poisonous to deer as in related *Laburnum*, and deer may also be repelled by the leaves.

HOW TO GROW

Site bush clovers where they will get sun for most of the day. They do best in lean, deep, sandy soil that drains freely. Like most pea family members, bush clovers root deeply and resent being moved, so choose their spot carefully. Fertilize only where the soil is very poor. Space 6 ft. or more apart if planting several. Since the stems are eye-catching in winter, delay spring pruning until silky new growth appears in midspring. Cut the woody base 6 to 12 in. above ground to control the height and girth of the plant.

DESIGN TIPS

Bush clovers leaf out late and need an attractive planting beneath them for spring in mixed plantings. Shade-loving coral bells (*Heuchera*) are a perfect choice; choose a dark-

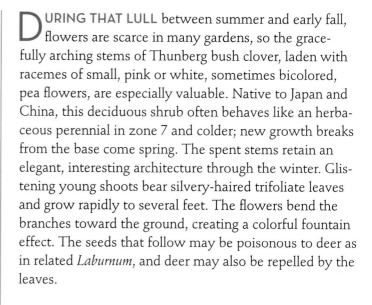

QUICK LOOK

Hardiness
Zones 6–8
Height and spread
6–7 ft. × 7–9 ft.
Deer resistance rating
9–10

A white-flowering cultivar of Thunberg bush clover (*Lespedeza thunbergii* 'White Fountain'). Photo by judywhite/GardenPhotos.com.

leaved selection such as 'Blackcurrant', 'Amethyst Mist', or 'Frosty Violet' (in warm climates) to play off against the silvery young foliage and flowers later on. If the bush clover is a focal point in the bed, annuals and perennials in shades of pink or magenta would be attractive companions. Try a grouping of 'Siskiyou Pink' gaura (*Gaura lindheimeri* 'Siskiyou Pink'), perhaps in combination with rose verbena (*Verbena canadensis*). In shrub collections, bush clover shows off well against evergreen boxwood (*Buxus*) or Japanese andromeda (*Pieris japonica*). An evergreen groundcover such as Russian cypress (*Microbiota decussata*) also provides good contrast. If soil is on the acid side, plant pink- or white-flowered heaths (*Erica*) and heathers (*Calluna*) beyond the drip line. Sun-loving companion shrubs might include bush cinquefoil (*Potentilla fruticosa* 'Princess' or 'Abbotswood'), *Weigela* Fine Wine ('Bramwell'), and glossy abelia (*Abelia* ×*grandiflora*) 'Silver Anniversary'. Thunberg bush clover's weeping habit makes it ideal for tumbling over walls or banks so that the flowers can be enjoyed from below. It also attracts butterflies and other insects, making it perfect for butterfly and wildlife gardens.

Bright pink-magenta 'Gibraltar' is a popular selection. 'Pink Fountain' is aptly named; in late summer it becomes a dense, silvery pink fountain of flowers, which last for several weeks if night temperatures are cool. 'Albiflora' and 'White Fountain' have pure white flowers; the latter blooms somewhat later and displays yellow fall color. Tolerant of light shade, 'Edo Shibori' has bicolored, white and pink flowers.

Its weeping habit makes it ideal for tumbling over walls or banks so that the flowers can be enjoyed from below.

Weigela

Weigela florida

ALTHOUGH WEIGELA was once thought of as an old-fashioned shrub found overgrown and neglected in gardens of abandoned homes, it has regained its popularity with the arrival of superior compact selections and cultivars. Many of these plants have colorful foliage that provides extended interest beyond their brief bloom time. Deer apparently find the foliage unpalatable, as browse damage is seldom apparent, although flower buds are occasionally eaten. Native along woodland edges in eastern Asia, it is tough and easy to grow.

This large shrub makes a real statement while in bloom. Its arching branches are weighed down with masses of 1½-in long, funnel-shaped, white, red, or pink flowers in early summer; rebloom is usually light. The hummingbird- and butterfly-attracting flowers, in groups of three or four, are carried on short new growths from the old wood. The oblong leaves, which may reach 4 in. long, blend into the background after bloom time. However, cultivars such as Wine and Roses ('Alexandra') and 'Java Red' (also called 'Folius Purpureis') have purple-red or bronzy foliage that is colorful through the season. Likewise, 'Variegata', with irregularly creamy or yellowish leaf margins, remains eye-catching.

HOW TO GROW

Depending upon the ultimate girth of the selection, plant weigelas 2 to 6 ft. apart. Full sun or light shade suits them, although intense southern sun may burn variegated forms. Good drainage is essential, but otherwise reasonably fertile soil suffices. Weigela appears unaffected by the pollution found in urban gardens. Remove dead wood at any time, but prune to shape and for renewal after flowering.

QUICK LOOK

Hardiness
Zones 4–9
Height and spread
1–9 ft. × 3–8 ft.
Deer resistance rating
8–10

DESIGN TIPS

Weigelas are perfect candidates for shrub or mixed borders. Large, green-leaved selections such as 'Pink Princess'
(5 to 6 ft. tall), 'Red Prince' (5 to 6 ft. tall), and 'Bristol
Ruby' (7 ft. tall) are best toward the back of the border,
perhaps alongside lilacs (*Syringa*) and later-blooming
abelia. Tall selections make colorful informal hedging, too.
Plant 3- to 4-ft. tall Carnaval ('Courtalour') where its pink
flower buds can bloom to display an unusual mix of pink,
red, and white flowers. Spider flowers (*Cleome*) in shades
of pink and purple combine well, along with poppies and
bleeding hearts (*Dicentra*). Maroon-leaved, 12- to 18-in.
Midnight Wine ('Elvera') makes an impact at the front of
the border with *Artemisia* 'Powis Castle' and German iris
(*Iris ×germanica*). Compact, dark-foliaged 'Minuet' has yel-
low-throated ruby flowers; it reblooms well. My Monet
('Verweig') is a petite weigela ideal for rock gardens. Its
grayish green leaves, tinged with pink when young, are
irregularly edged with cream; they accent the large, pink
funnel flowers to perfection. Not confined to rock gardens, My Monet does well in containers and makes a fine
low specimen, too. Yellow-leaved shrubs always demand
attention as specimens, and Ghost ('Carlton') weigela is
no exception. This 4- to 5-ft. tall selection has chartreuse
foliage in spring that matures to pale butter yellow in
summer, in striking contrast to its blood red flowers. Try a
skirt of lady's mantle beneath. The 2- to 3-ft. tall novelty
'Eyecatcher' is well named, with deep red flowers and
foliage irregularly edged in bold yellow; it is suitable for
containers as well as the landscape.

Ghost ('Carlton') weigela has chartreuse foliage in spring that matures to pale butter yellow in summer, in striking contrast to its blood red flowers.

Weigela florida Wine and Roses ('Alexandra').

Ferns

Japanese painted fern (*Athyrium niponicum*), maidenhair fern (*Adiantum*), and astilbe thrive in similar shaded places.

Autumn fern

Dryopteris erythrosora

THIS STUNNING evergreen or semievergreen fern demands a place in shaded gardens, especially for the shiny copper-orange young growth described by its alternate common name, Japanese red shield fern. The mature fronds are also shiny but are bright green, giving the plant a bicolored effect, especially in spring. The triangular fronds are cut into twice-divided pinnae. Their undersides are dotted with red or pink, kidney-shaped indusia that protect the spores—hence yet another common name, pink shield fern. Perhaps these and the texture of autumn fern are what deter deer.

HOW TO GROW

Found in the wild in China, Taiwan, and Japan, autumn fern thrives in part shade with rich, slightly acid soil that retains moisture. Intense sun tends to scorch the fronds and is not tolerated well. Given sufficient moisture, autumn fern grows well under deciduous trees, especially oaks (*Dryopteris* means "oak fern") and beeches. It is not a tidy grower, with fronds emerging from the crown in every direction, giving it a slightly wild look. Cut back any scruffy-looking leaves, especially after the winter. Even in warm climates where it is evergreen, a little grooming may be necessary. Autumn fern spreads slowly by scaly rhizomes but is by no means invasive. Plant in humus-rich soil about 15 in. apart, in groups to make an impact. It is important not to plant too deeply; the crown should be at ground level. This fern is quite susceptible to air pollution, so if it does well for you, you can rest assured that your air quality is good.

QUICK LOOK

Hardiness
Zones 4–9
Height and spread
1–2 ft. × 1–3 ft.
Deer resistance rating
9–10

Autumn fern (*Dryopteris erythrosora*).

This cheerful fern is certainly eye-catching in spring and continues to appeal throughout the year.

DESIGN TIPS

This cheerful fern is certainly eye-catching in spring and continues to appeal throughout the year. It can fill many a spot in the garden and is outstanding beneath deep-rooted hickories (*Carya*) and black tupelo (*Nyssa sylvatica*), where it combines well with shade-loving bulbs and perennials such as snowdrops (*Galanthus*), summer snowflakes (*Leucojum*), foamflowers (*Tiarella*), bigroot geranium (*Geranium macrorrhizum*), hellebores (*Helleborus*), and leatherleaf sedge (*Carex buchananii*). In a lightly shaded mixed border, plant groups of autumn fern with daffodils and coral bells (*Heuchera*), especially apricot-leaved cultivars such as 'Amber Waves', 'Crème Brûlée', and 'Peach Melba'. As a backdrop try shrubby 'Goldflame' Japanese spirea (*Spiraea japonica* 'Goldflame'), which has orangey young foliage to echo the new fern growth. Wintercreeper (*Euonymus fortunei* 'Emerald 'n' Gold') also makes a nice companion for autumn fern, along with leucothoe (*Leucothoe axillaris*). Avoid the popular 'Rainbow' drooping leucothoe (*L. fontanesiana* 'Rainbow'), which deer heavily browse according to several reports.

'Brilliance' is a showy cultivar with much brighter orange color said to remain on the fronds as they reach maturity. An ideal container plant for a very lightly shaded spot on a terrace or patio, 'Brilliance' might be combined with trailing golden creeping Jenny (*Lysimachia nummularia* 'Aurea') and golden pineapple sage (*Salvia elegans* 'Golden Delicious') for a monochromatic design. Lacy autumn fern (*Dryopteris erythrosora* 'Prolifica', zones 6 to 9) has a cascading habit and the same brilliant coppery young growth, though the leaves are more deeply cut. It might be attractive in a hanging basket as a specimen plant.

Christmas fern

Polystichum acrostichoides

IN WINTER in the moist, rocky woodlands of the North-east, the deep green, evergreen foliage of Christmas ferns stands out. The plants retain their color all season long in spite of winter rains and snow. In Victorian times the fronds were cut and used for Christmas decorations. Florists now often use them in winter arrangements.

Christmas fern produces fertile and sterile fronds, the former somewhat longer and encircled by the latter. The glossy, leathery, sword-shaped fronds, widest in the middle, are cut once into toothed, boot-shaped leaflets, whimsically reminiscent of Christmas stockings. Spores are borne only on the small upper pinnae of the fertile fronds. After releasing the spores, these tips often drop off.

Old fronds of Christmas fern provide cover for wildlife, including wild turkey. Deer and bear very occasionally browse the young fiddleheads, but mature leaves, which are rough in texture and contain chemicals distasteful to deer, are seldom browsed.

HOW TO GROW

Christmas fern thrives in the shade but also tolerates modest sun in northern gardens. Plant young ferns 2 ft. apart just below soil level and keep well watered until they become established. After the winter, remove shabby old fronds to expose the beautiful new fiddleheads. Christmas ferns are best massed in groups in the landscape, as they would occur in nature. They are not fussy about soil, although moist, humus-rich places are ideal. Dryer rocky spots and difficult banks are also appropriate where the ferns help to control erosion. Young fiddleheads, silvery with scales, rise from a multiple-crowned

QUICK LOOK

Hardiness
Zones 3–9
Height and spread
1–1½ ft. × 1 ft.
Deer resistance rating
8–10

rootstock. Simple division of the crowns produces more plants.

DESIGN TIPS

In woodlands, combine Christmas fern with native wild-flowers such as spring-blooming bloodroot (*Sanguinaria canadensis*), Canadian wild ginger (*Asarum canadense*), and wild geranium (*Geranium maculatum*); white wood aster (*Aster divaricatus*) is a good fall partner. Spicebush (*Lindera benzoin*) and shadbush (*Amelanchier canadensis*) are suitable native woody companions. In shaded garden borders, plant it with coral bells (*Heuchera*), barrenworts (*Epimedium*), and fringed bleeding heart (*Dicentra eximia*) beneath winter hazel (*Corylopsis*), forsythia, and summersweet (*Clethra*). Later-blooming bugbanes (*Actaea*), monkshoods (*Aconitum*), and astilbes provide more color. Along shaded driveways and paths, interplant groups of Christmas fern with sweet woodruff (*Galium odoratum*) and Allegheny spurge (*Pachysandra procumbens*) for a lovely foliage contrast. Intermittent groupings of Christmas fern attract the eye, adding height, texture, and interest to existing mass plantings of Japanese spurge (*Pachysandra terminalis*). Perhaps on the north side of the house, consider planting spotted-leaved lungworts (*Pulmonaria*) or variegated Hakone grass (*Hakonechloa macra* 'Aureola') with Christmas fern for an easy-care foundation.

Decorative variants of Christmas fern include 'Cristatum', with crested tips to the fronds, and frilly-edged 'Crispum'. Similar but slightly smaller, native western sword fern (*Polystichum munitum*) is best for western gardens. Braun's holly fern (*P. braunii*), Makinoi's holly fern (*P. makinoi*), and several related holly ferns are also fine garden items.

In Victorian times the fronds were cut and used for Christmas decorations. Florists now often use them in winter arrangements.

Christmas fern (*Polystichum acrostichoides*).

Cinnamon fern

Osmunda cinnamomea

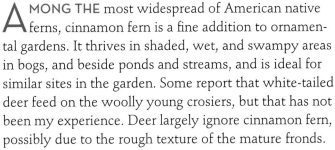

AMONG THE most widespread of American native ferns, cinnamon fern is a fine addition to ornamental gardens. It thrives in shaded, wet, and swampy areas in bogs, and beside ponds and streams, and is ideal for similar sites in the garden. Some report that white-tailed deer feed on the woolly young crosiers, but that has not been my experience. Deer largely ignore cinnamon fern, possibly due to the rough texture of the mature fronds.

Cinnamon ferns emerge early in the season. Densely hairy crosiers rise from stout, wiry rootstocks (widely harvested for orchid growing) and unfurl to green, spore-bearing fronds. After shedding their spores, they turn a beautiful rusty cinnamon brown but die back in early summer. Arching, sterile fronds produce vase-shaped plants when mature; the bright green fronds are twice divided, tufted with hairs along the midrib (rachis) and stipe (stem). These remain on the plant until the first autumn frosts. The rhizomes or creeping stems grow slowly from dense black rootstocks and spread into large stands over time.

HOW TO GROW

Damp, acid soil and a shaded site are optimum, but cinnamon ferns tolerate some sun if kept moist. In spring or early summer plant clumps 2 ft. or so apart with the crowns just above soil level; add a mulch of compost or shredded bark to retain moisture. Propagate by dividing the rootstocks and keep well watered until they are established. Pests and diseases seldom attack this easy-to-grow, low-maintenance fern.

QUICK LOOK

Hardiness
Zones 2–10
Height and spread
2½–5 ft. × 1½ ft.
Deer resistance rating
8–10

Cinnamon fern (*Osmunda cinnamomea*).

Densely hairy crosiers rise from stout, wiry rootstocks and unfurl to green, spore-bearing fronds.

DESIGN TIPS

In damp woodlands, plant cinnamon ferns with drifts of forget-me-nots (*Myosotis*), summer snowflake (*Leucojum aestivum*), and Canada mayflower (*Maianthemum canadense*) at their feet. 'Brazen Hussy' lesser celandine (*Ranunculus ficaria* 'Brazen Hussy') is also interesting as a spring-blooming groundcover, but avoid the species, which is very invasive. Woodland shrub companions might include summersweet (*Clethra alnifolia*) and its cultivars. Succulent young growth may be browsed sometimes, so get tall shrubs that will be out of reach. Winterberry (*Ilex verticillata*) is another good woody companion. The yellowing fall fronds of cinnamon fern are a delightful contrast to reddening winterberry berries. Either of these shrubs is appropriate in a native plant garden, along with spring-blooming shadbush (*Amelanchier canadensis*) and spicebush (*Lindera benzoin*). Columbines (*Aquilegia*), red baneberry (*Actaea rubra*), turtleheads (*Chelone*), and black snakeroot (*Actaea racemosa*) are all suitable native companions and provide color during the season. In wildlife gardens cinnamon fern provides cover for birds, and "fern down" that blue- and ruby-throated hummingbirds gather to line their nests. In damp, lightly shaded borders Siberian iris (*Iris sibirica*) and Japanese iris (*I. ensata*) provide later color after summer snowflake and quamash (*Camassia*) are finished blooming. Sedges (*Carex*), including mace sedge (*C. grayi*) and hop sedge (*C. lupulina*), provide textural contrast.

Royal fern (*Osmunda regalis*) and interrupted fern (*O. claytoniana*) also make good ornamentals for the garden. Royal fern takes even wetter conditions and creates wiry tussocks. It tolerates full sun in the North if kept moist. Interrupted fern prefers drier soil.

Japanese painted fern

Athyrium niponicum

*A*THYRIUM NIPONICUM, also known as *A. goering-ianum*, is perhaps the most decorative of cultivated ferns, and various selections are widely grown in gardens across the United States. The species, which is mostly green, is native to shaded places in eastern Asia and is seldom grown. However, the best-known cultivar, 'Pictum', was selected as Perennial Plant of the Year in 2004 by the Perennial Plant Association, which indicates its popularity as well as its reliability as a garden plant. Deer seem to dislike the texture of the fern foliage.

All the lady ferns (*Athyrium*) are easy to grow, deciduous, and hardy in temperate regions; Japanese painted fern is the showiest and most colorful of the group. Its beautiful, twice-divided, triangular fronds are a metallic grayish green flushed with purplish maroon along the rachis and veins. The fronds hold their color well all season long but are particularly bright in cool weather. New young growth keeps coming.

HOW TO GROW

Creeping rhizomes spread freely but not aggressively in light or part shade, preferably where soil is acid, loose, and moist. In spring and fall apply a 2- to 3-in. mulch of compost to maintain soil texture and moisture. Cut back old growth after the first frost or leave it for spring shearing. In spring be careful not to damage the tightly furled crosier tips. Propagate by division in early spring. Plants can be started from spores but may take several years to become sizeable.

QUICK LOOK

Hardiness
Zones 4–9
Height and spread
1–2 ft. × 2 ft.
Deer resistance rating
9–10

DESIGN TIPS

Many selections of Japanese painted fern have appeared in the marketplace. Similar in size and habit to 'Pictum', 'Pewter Lace' has unusual pewter gray fronds accented with deepest purple stems. Plant either about 1 ft. apart for a dense groundcover or intermingle with lily-of-the-valley (*Convallaria majalis*), Allegheny foamflower (*Tiarella cordifolia*), or other groundcovers. For limited space, 'Burgundy Lace' makes neat 1-ft. tall clumps. Its purple young growth is veined with silver, but mature fronds are silvery green veined with purple. Compact 'Silver Falls' has more delicate, light silvery green fronds. Plant this one close, perhaps to illuminate the edge of a woodland path, or use it as a focal point in a shady rock garden. 'Ursula's Red' has a weeping habit, while ruffled 'Regal Red' produces a fluffy effect. 'Ghost', a 36-in. tall hybrid, is elegant massed as a tall groundcover in woodlands, or beneath silverbells (*Halesia*), dogwoods (*Cornus*), and other trees and shrubs. Its upright, light green fronds overlaid with silver give a ghostly effect. Crested 'Applecourt' is distinctive enough for a stand-alone container.

What to plant with Japanese painted fern? Silver-spotted lungworts (*Pulmonaria*) and coral bells (*Heuchera*) come to mind. Choose purple- or maroon-leaved selections of coral bells, such as 'Plum Pudding' or 'Blackcurrant' (Dolce series), to echo the purple variegation in the ferns. Barrenwort (*Epimedium*) is another good choice. Its heart-shaped leaves on wiry stems contrast in texture and shape with delicate fern fronds throughout the season. Red barrenwort (*E. ×rubrum*) is especially appropriate, as its young, fresh green leaves are edged and veined in red.

Its beautiful, twice-divided, triangular fronds are a metallic grayish green flushed with purplish maroon along the rachis and veins.

Japanese painted fern (*Athyrium niponicum* 'Pictum').

Ostrich fern

Matteuccia struthiopteris

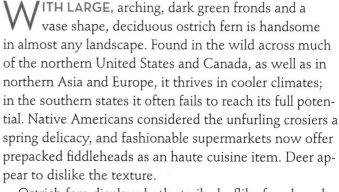

WITH LARGE, arching, dark green fronds and a vase shape, deciduous ostrich fern is handsome in almost any landscape. Found in the wild across much of the northern United States and Canada, as well as in northern Asia and Europe, it thrives in cooler climates; in the southern states it often fails to reach its full potential. Native Americans considered the unfurling crosiers a spring delicacy, and fashionable supermarkets now offer prepacked fiddleheads as an haute cuisine item. Deer appear to dislike the texture.

Ostrich fern displays both sterile, leaflike fronds and stiff, fertile ones that bear spores. Arising from a thick, upright rootstock, the fiddleheads emerge in early spring, densely covered with woolly hairs (remove these if you plan on eating them). They grow vigorously, even to 6 ft. long and 1 ft. wide, with pairs of cut leaflets. In midsummer the fertile fronds appear encircled by the sterile ones. Green at first, they turn brown and become woody after the spores are released. They remain on the plant all winter and are valuable additions to winter arrangements.

HOW TO GROW

Plant ostrich ferns at least 2 to 3 ft. apart in moist, humus-rich soil that seldom dries out. An organic mulch is beneficial. Avoid windy places. This plant does not demand wet conditions and tolerates even dryish shade, though in this situation it will never attain its full elegant beauty.

Ostrich fern spreads by slender underground stems. Under favorable conditions, these can result in large colonies over time. Some consider this plant invasive, but more often it spreads in a controllable manner. Remove the new young plants to propagate them, and replant

QUICK LOOK

Hardiness
Zones 2–6
Height and spread
2–6 ft. × 2 ft.
Deer resistance rating
9–10

Ostrich fern (*Matteuccia struthiopteris*).

With large, arching, dark green fronds and a vase shape, deciduous ostrich fern is handsome in almost any landscape.

so that the crowns are just at or slightly above soil level. Keep them well watered until established.

DESIGN TIPS

These easy-care ferns provide an excellent backdrop in light or deeper shade for mixed borders, and native or wild gardens. They may be used in foundation plantings if moisture is sufficient. In a garden setting ostrich ferns mix well with shrubs, perennials, and other flowering plants. Their bold, stand-alone presence also sets off garden orna-ments or sculpture well, drawing the eye to the subject without overwhelming it. Solo, in a substantial decorative container, ostrich fern commands an exotic presence. A pair of containers at the entrance to a shaded garden could be dramatic. In mixed beds and borders select shade-lov-ing companions for ostrich fern. Hellebores (*Helleborus*), lungworts (*Pulmonaria*), barrenworts (*Epimedium*), coral bells (*Heuchera*), and bugbanes (*Actaea*) are all suitable companions. Variegated Hakone grass (*Hakonechloa macra* 'Aureola') is an especially elegant partner, contrasting in texture and color with the fern. In lightly shaded native gardens or woodlands, plant ostrich fern beneath flower-ing dogwood (*Cornus florida*), spicebush (*Lindera benzoin*), summersweet (*Clethra alnifolia*), or shadbush (*Amelanchier canadensis*). Canada columbines (*Aquilegia canadensis*), mayapples (*Podophyllum peltatum*), turtleheads (*Chelone*), and white wood aster (*Aster divaricatus*) provide floral in-terest during the season. For an appealing foliage contrast, try low-growing Allegheny spurge (*Pachysandra procum-bens*), a seldom-seen, deer-resistant native with attractive mottled leaves and pinkish flowers in spring. It is a clump-ing plant, not as aggressive as its Japanese cousin.

Bulbs

The rounded heads of 'Globemaster' ornamental onion (*Allium* 'Globemaster') stand out dramatically against deep blue Siberian iris (*Iris sibirica*).

Daffodil

Narcissus species and cultivars

DAFFODILS, narcissus, jonquils—by any name, these glorious flowers can be the backbone of deer-tolerant gardens in spring, especially where winters are cold. They come in a range of sizes, their flowers yellow, white, pink, orange, or a combination of these. Many use the term "daffodils" to refer particularly to the large, golden yellow trumpets of varieties such as 'King Alfred' and 'Dutch Master', but it is also a catch-all. "Narcissus" comes from the Latin genus name, and "jonquil" refers to those plants derived from *Narcissus jonquilla*, but both are also used in the vernacular. This diverse group has been divided into twelve parts based on flower characteristics. All contain poisonous alkaloids that affect deer. (For more in-depth information, refer to Brent and Becky Heath's *Daffodils for North American Gardens*.)

HOW TO GROW
Rich, well-drained soil is ideal for daffodils. The bulbs may rot in wet soils; for better drainage, plant in raised beds or on a hillside. Amend less-than-perfect soils with thoroughly rotted compost, leaves, or animal manure. Plant the bulbs nose up in fall, in a hole roughly three times as deep as their diameter (about 6 to 8 in. deep for large bulbs, 3 to 6 in. for medium ones, and 2 to 3 in. for small ones). Water the bulbs well, mulch, and keep moist until the ground freezes.

DESIGN TIPS
There is a narcissus for almost every spot in the garden. Use early small ones, such as golden 'Tête-à-tête' and 'Little Beauty' in rock gardens, along with Grecian windflower (*Anemone blanda*), Siberian squills (*Scilla sibirica*),

QUICK LOOK

Hardiness
Zones 3–9
Height and spread
6–30 in. × 12 in.
Deer resistance rating
9–10

'Quail' jonquilla daffodil (*Narcissus* 'Quail').

Larger daffodils massed and blooming at the base of a hedge, wall, or fence are an awesome sight.

and rock cress (*Aubrieta ×cultorum*). Larger daffodils ('Salome', 'Mt. Hood', and 'Ceylon' are good ones) massed and blooming at the base of a hedge, wall, or fence are an awesome sight. They are also spectacular blanketing a hillside, perhaps bordered with fragrant winter hazel (*Corylopsis glabrescens*) or later-blooming Japanese andromeda (*Pieris japonica*). Midseason 'Quail' bears up to four fragrant, golden flowers on each sturdy stem; just taller than the reedlike leaves, they stand out well in the landscape. Avoid planting daffodils where livestock may ingest them. If early, midseason, and late varieties are used to extend the bloom time, group each variety in a drift for the most impact. Informal lawn or meadow plantings are beautiful, but daffodil foliage must not be cut until it has fully ripened (about six weeks after bloom). In formal beds where ripening foliage is unsightly, the bulbs may be lifted and put in a shaded trench over the summer to ripen before replanting in fall. Ideally, plant later-developing perennials (hardy geraniums, hybrid sage, and false indigo, for example) to camouflage dying foliage, or plant summer annuals among it. Many daffodil bulbs, in addition to paperwhites ('Cragford', 'Pipit', and 'Ice Follies', for instance), force well for early flowers indoors. Those hardy in your zone can be ripened off and planted out in the garden for bloom next year. Plant them at the base of trees and shrubs where they will bloom for years to come. Winter jasmine (*Jasminum nudiflorum*) and forsythia are good companions, although some report that deer occasionally browse forsythia flowers.

Lily leek

Allium moly

ORNAMENTAL ONIONS are widely used in gardens because they have wonderful flowers and are disliked by deer, who apparently do not find onion breath sexy. Lily leek, also known as golden garlic, is an outstanding example. The bulbs are edible, as are the flowers, which make attractive garnishes for salads if you can spare them from the garden.

In Greek mythology, moly was a mythical herb that grew in the Elysian Fields. The botanical name refers to this plant's reputation for having magical powers—lily leeks are still grown by some to bring prosperity and good luck. To gardeners in deer country, perhaps the magic is that deer leave it alone. Planted in fall, it is slow to emerge in spring. Each bulb produces a pair of dusty green, tulip-like leaves that die neatly soon after bloom time. Loose, 2-in. wide umbels of sparkling gold, starry flowers appear on naked stems by early summer. Attractive to butterflies and hummingbirds, the flowers are fine for cutting, although they have a slight oniony smell. 'Jeannine' is an improvement on the species, slightly taller and blooming a week or so later.

HOW TO GROW

This low-maintenance bulb hails from Spain and southwestern Europe where the soil drains freely and it is not subjected to waterlogged soil in winter. It does best in sunny or lightly shaded spots in rock gardens, grouped at the front of shrub or perennial borders, or naturalized in substantial drifts. The bulbs produce offsets and reproduce freely by seed if not deadheaded.

QUICK LOOK

Hardiness
Zones 3–9
Height and spread
12–15 in. × 12 in.
Deer resistance rating
8–10

DESIGN TIPS

The huge ornamental onion clan includes plants that range from 6 in. to 5 ft. tall, with flowers in white, yellow, lavender, blue, pink, and purple. Decorate spring rock gardens with lily leek and the softball-size heads of silvery white flowers and broad, arching leaves of Turkestan onion (*Allium karataviense*). Myrtle euphorbia (*Euphorbia myrsinites*) and woolly thyme (*Thymus pseudolanuginosus*) are appropriate companions. In summer, lilac German garlic (*Allium senescens*) and deep pink prairie onion (*A. stellatum*) mix well with hummingbird mints (*Agastache*), yellow corydalis (*Corydalis lutea*), and hardy geraniums. Edge herb and vegetable gardens with chives (*Allium schoenoprasum*) and parsley. In wild meadows or native plant gardens, consider 18-in. nodding onion (*A. cernuum*). Clumps of this self-seeder with drooping lavender-pink flowers are charming among native grasses in late summer. The most dramatic ornamental onions display huge spherical heads of flowers, some as large as softballs. Giant onion (*A. giganteum*) hoists its deep lilac, 4-in. flower globes to 4 or 5 ft. on stiff, naked stems. Plant these bulbs in threes or fives at the back of the border or among shrubs. Less dramatic but still eye-catching *A.* 'Globemaster' and *A.* 'Ambassador' are also popular. Several species with small, inexpensive bulbs (plant lots of them) are good cut flowers and interesting companions for perennials and low shrubs. Imagine the tight, deep blue umbels of blue globe onion (*A. caeruleum*) with Siberian iris or wood spurge (*Euphorbia amygdaloides*), or the dense, deep purple heads of drumstick allium (*A. sphaerocephalon*) planted among pink peonies.

The bulbs are edible, as are the flowers, which make attractive garnishes for salads if you can spare them from the garden.

Lily leek (*Allium moly*).

Snowdrop

Galanthus nivalis

SNOWDROPS ARE the harbingers of spring, sometimes even piercing late-winter snow with their flower-bud-tipped stems. Judging by their place in poetry and other literature, they have been held dear by humans throughout the ages. Deer, however, seem to find their gooey sap unpleasant.

The 1-in. flowers emerge from bud on slender, swinging stems and consist of three all-white, long outer segments. The three inner segments are shorter, notched at the tips and marked with emerald green. They exude a light fragrance, especially on sunny days, to attract pollinating insects. Most bulbs produce a pair of slender leaves that elongate as they mature.

HOW TO GROW

Snowdrops are native throughout much of Europe and are protected from wild collection by CITES (Convention on International Trade in Endangered Species of Wild Fauna and Flora); always check that the bulbs you buy are nursery propagated. They are perennial, growing from bulbs that are planted in fall, and do best in cool climates, seldom lasting well in the South. Snowdrops prefer a position in sun or part shade where the soil drains well but remains evenly moist. However, they tolerate dry soils well and readily naturalize under deep-rooted deciduous trees and in woodlands. Plant them about 3 in. deep and several inches from each other as the bulbs produce offsets. After about five years the bulbs become crowded; lift them right after bloom time while the leaves are still "in the green," and pry the bulbs apart prior to immediate replanting. Seed capsules develop readily as well, if early

QUICK LOOK

Hardiness
Zones 3–7
Height and spread
6–9 in. × 12 in.
Deer resistance rating
9–10

Snowdrop (*Galanthus nivalis*).

Drifts or patches
of hundreds of
snowdrops are
spectacular at the
feet of trees and
shrubs.

foraging bees have visited and pollinated the flowers. Ants distribute the seeds.

DESIGN TIPS

Although the common snowdrop is the most widely grown, several cultivars and other species are available. 'S. Arnott' has larger, very fragrant flowers. The double form 'Flore Pleno' has green-marked, frilly inner segments. 'Viridiapicis' is somewhat taller, green-marked on the inside and with a large green patch on the outer tips. Giant snowdrop (*Galanthus elwesii*) may reach 12 in. tall and blooms slightly later. The 1- to 2-in. outer segments flare open, revealing the inner segments, which are banded and tipped with green. They are very fragrant.

Plant as many snowdrops as you can afford; the small bulbs are inexpensive except for some rarities. Drifts or patches of hundreds of snowdrops are spectacular at the feet of trees and shrubs. They can be planted among ferns, with bear's foot hellebores (*Helleborus foetidus*), Lenten roses (*H. orientalis*), coral bells, and many other shade-loving perennials. Plant clumps of them in rock gardens among evergreen moss pink (*Phlox subulata*) and winter heath (*Erica carnea*). Avoid planting snowdrop bulbs among Japanese spurge (*Pachysandra terminalis*), as it is too greedy to support other plants. Snowdrops should return year after year, but in hot climates they may not perennialize well.

Container plantings give you the chance to get up close and personal without crawling around on hands and knees. Create a miniature-bulb garden in a half-barrel along with cultivars of netted iris (*Iris reticulata*)—'Cantab' is pale blue, 'Harmony' is deep blue, both with yellow blotches on the falls. Add trailing large vinca (*Vinca major*) to soften the edge.

Summer snowflake

Leucojum aestivum

FROM A DISTANCE summer snowflakes look like tall snowdrops (*Galanthus*), and they are just as welcome in my garden. The dangling, green-tipped, white bells open in late spring (not in summer as the name suggests—loddon lily is another, better, common name) depending what region they are grown in. At any time, this beauty is valuable for its easy-care ways and long bloom time. Deer find the gelatinous sap unpleasant.

Summer snowflake has become naturalized in parts of the eastern United States and Canada as well as in California and Oregon; it is native in much of central and southern Europe. The bulbs are poisonous to small mammals, so mice, voles, and chipmunks usually leave them alone. Each hollow stem bears several flowers, with inner and outer segments the same length, blotched with pea green at the tips. Each bulb produces a few dark green, ½-in. wide leaves that remain until midsummer. The flowers are good as cut flowers and last a week or so in water. Condition them as you would daffodils. The sap causes skin irritation in some people, so gloves may be needed when handling them.

HOW TO GROW

The bulbs look like small daffodil bulbs and should be planted in fall about 3 to 5 in. deep and several inches apart in sun or part shade. They produce offsets and gradually build large colonies if not disturbed. Lift bulbs only when they become crowded, usually after three or more years; separate clumps and replant them while still in leaf. If they are not increasing much, they may be drying out in summer or could be planted too deep.

QUICK LOOK

Hardiness
Zones 4–8
Height and spread
12–18 in. × 12 in.
Deer resistance rating
9–10

DESIGN TIPS

Summer snowflakes are at their best growing in rough grassland or in a meadow garden. They thrive where the soil remains damp in bog gardens and along the banks of streams and ponds, but the bulbs do not actually grow in water. Spreading yellow flag iris (*Iris pseudacorus*) is an attractive companion in wet places but is on some exotic invasives lists across the United States, so check before planting. Drifts of forget-me-nots (*Myosotis*) blooming beneath summer snowflakes present a charming picture that will return each spring as the forget-me-nots reseed themselves. In drier soils, early-blooming cultivars of Siberian iris (*Iris sibirica*) are good companions; cultivars such as deep blue 'Caesar's Brother' and lavender 'Dance Ballerina Dance' usually bloom at the same time as summer snowflake. Late-blooming daffodils and narcissus are fine partners, too. Snowflakes do better than snowdrops in the South. In February at the Beauregard-Keyes House in New Orleans, formal low boxwood hedges enclose parterre beds filled with summer snowflakes. What an elegant look! For high-profile places, it is wise to pay a little more for the robust and larger-flowered 'Gravetye Giant' for greater impact. In mixed gardens and among shrubs, plant summer snowflakes with a dark backdrop such as *Weigela* Midnight Wine ('Elvera') or evergreen Japanese holly (*Ilex crenata*). In very light woodlands many ferns, including cinnamon fern (*Osmunda cinnamomea*) and ostrich fern (*Matteuccia struthiopteris*), are just unfurling their spring green finery when summer snowflakes bloom.

This beauty is valuable for its easy-care ways and long bloom time.

Summer snowflake (*Leucojum aestivum*).

171

'Waterlily' autumn crocus

Colchicum 'Waterlily'

'WATERLILY' AUTUMN CROCUS isn't a crocus at all, but it does bloom in fall. Though crocuslike, colchicums differ from crocuses on several counts, including the lack of a white line down the center of each leaf, and having six rather than three stamens. They are also poisonous to deer and rodents. Of garden origin, 'Waterlily' is one of a group of hybrids derived from several species, including showy colchicum (*Colchicum speciosum*). Its double, pinkish lavender flowers rise from a lopsided corm. Narrow, 12-in. tall, food-producing leaves appear in spring, later dying back as temperatures heat up. The flowers bloom without foliage and are best growing through groundcover that can keep them from falling over. In a wild spot at Blithewold Mansion, Rhode Island, a memorable planting of 'Waterlily' and other colchicums grow in light shade through variegated bishop's weed (*Aegopodium podagraria* 'Variegata'). Where space is not limited, this combination makes an impressive display.

HOW TO GROW

Plant the corms as soon as possible in late summer. If you keep them in a box or bag for more than a few days, you may be surprised to find them in full bloom without water or light. Plant each in light shade about 4 in. deep and 8 in. apart in well-drained soil. They tolerate drought well. After three or four years, lift and divide the corms when dormant to avoid overcrowding. All parts of the plant are toxic to humans and other animals, so it is wise to wear gloves when handling the corms.

QUICK LOOK

Hardiness
Zones 4–8
Height and spread
6–8 in. × 6 in.
Deer resistance rating
9–10

'Waterlily' autumn crocus (*Colchicum* 'Waterlily').

In a wild spot at Blithewold Mansion, Rhode Island, a memorable planting of 'Waterlily' and other colchicums grow in light shade through variegated bishop's weed.

DESIGN TIPS

'Waterlily' naturalizes well in wild or meadow gardens and is attractive in rock gardens. It does well in containers, too, especially combined with purple-leaved coral bells (*Heuchera*) and lavender or white sweet alyssum (*Lobularia maritima*). Other colchicum hybrids of note include the late-blooming 'Lilac Wonder', whose 8-in., rosy mauve goblets tend to topple over with rain. Free-flowering 'The Giant' has rosy lilac flowers that are white at the base and up to 12 in. tall. The lightly mottled, deep purple flowers of 'Violet Queen' appear in late summer, as do those of meadow saffron (*Colchicum autumnale*), also known as naked boys. Their orchid-colored blooms are smaller than some, but there are more of them. A double white form, *C. autumnale* 'Alboplenum', is especially attractive. Showy colchicum produces several fragrant 4-in. flowers in varying shades of reddish violet as well as pure white (*C. speciosum* 'Album').

In the landscape a good effect can be produced using flowers of similar color. I remember one October at the Chicago Botanic Garden coming upon a sweep of lavender sweet alyssum (*Lobularia maritima*) with colchicum growing through it in full bloom. It was unforgettable. Late-blooming leadwort's (*Ceratostigma plumbaginoides*) purplish blue flowers with red calyces provide a colorful foil, particularly for 'Violet Queen'. 'Waterlily' has enough presence to show off among low ferns, such as dwarf forms of soft shield fern (*Polystichum setiferum*). This combination is suitable for a rock garden or at the base of a wall. In containers grow lavender or purple colchicum with trailing golden creeping Jenny (*Lysimachia nummularia* 'Aurea'), perhaps adding Luscious Grape ('Robpwpur') lantana to fill out the picture.

Herbs

Woolly thyme (*Thymus pseudolanuginosus*) blankets the
ground beneath lavender.

Basil

Ocimum basilicum

BASIL, also called sweet basil, is probably the most widely used herb in the United States and Canada. After all, what beats a fresh basil and homegrown tomato sandwich? Basil has been grown since the time of the ancient Greeks and is the stuff of folklore and myths through the ages. It is associated with fire-breathing dragons and sinister plots, erotic encounters, and sacred ceremonies across the globe. The strong-smelling essential oils in basil mostly protect it from deer, although damage has been reported.

There seem to be countless varieties of basil (some say upwards of 150), attesting to its popularity. Outside warm areas where they can be grown year-round, basils are treated as summer annuals. The essential oils are found in all parts of the plant but especially in the oval, usually 2-in. long leaves. These are mostly bright green, but cultivars with purple, frilly, or curled leaves are interesting alternatives. Different varieties have different aromas: anise, cinnamon, lime, and lemon. Basils are widely used in cooking, especially for making flavored vinegars, and in Italian dishes.

HOW TO GROW

Start seeds indoors in spring in strong light. Plant out seedlings only after all danger of frost has passed and soil has warmed. A position in full sun with well-drained, fertile soil gets best results. Successive sowings indoors or directly outdoors through the season will keep a steady supply of fragrant leaves coming on. Pinch the growing tips of young plants to encourage bushy growth and remove the white flowers (they make a pretty garnish) as soon as they appear to keep the plants strong.

QUICK LOOK

Hardiness
Zones 9–11
Height and spread
1–2 ft. × 1–2 ft.
Deer resistance rating
7–9

Three basils, *Ocimum basilicum* (top), *O. basilicum* 'Spicy Globe' (middle), and *O. basilicum* 'Siam Queen' (bottom).

Different varieties have different aromas: anise, cinnamon, lime, and lemon.

DESIGN TIPS

Every year it seems yet another basil variety comes on the market. Pretty, variegated 'Pesto Perpetuo', a 2- to 3-ft. nonblooming cultivar, offers lots of lime green leaves edged with cream. It is most attractive planted in flowerbeds with zinnias, marigolds, and bachelor's buttons (*Centaurea cyanus*). Bushy 'Citriodorum' basil has light green, lemony-smelling leaves, an appropriate garnish for fish dishes. If it is allowed to mature, its white flowers produce lemon-flavored seeds. 'Sweet Dani' also has a strong citrusy flavor. 'Mammoth Sweet' has slightly puckered, very large, yellow-green leaves coveted by Italian chefs. Compact 'Spicy Globe' has very small leaves and is perfect as a windowsill plant or to edge a bed in herb, vegetable, or even rock gardens. Licorice-flavored 'Siam Queen', with purple flowers, is much in demand due to the popularity of Thai cuisine. Among purple-leaved varieties is lavender-flowered 'Red Rubin', which holds its color well through the season and is popular in Middle Eastern cooking for its sharp flavor. Partner frilly-leaved 'Purple Ruffles' with yellow-leaved bluebeard (*Caryopteris incana* Sunshine Blue) in the garden, or grow it alone in large containers. In the landscape, purple-leaved varieties have the most impact. Try a group of 'Osmin Purple' with lamb's ears (*Stachys byzantina*) at its feet, perhaps accompanied by 'Moonshine' yarrow (*Achillea millefolium* 'Moonshine') or dusty miller (*Senecio cineraria*). In Budapest large tubs planted with 4-ft. tall, blooming 'African Blue' basil are sometimes set outside bars and restaurants to attract patrons. In herb containers, add chives, thyme, and 'Tricolor' sage (*Salvia officinalis* 'Tricolor') to basil for an attractive mix.

Greek oregano

Origanum vulgare subsp. hirtum

GREEK OREGANO is a subspecies of wild marjoram, another Mediterranean herb that delights in lots of sun and sweet, well-drained soil. The species is not very flavorful, but subspecies *hirtum* has a spicy, pungent smell well known to pizza lovers and hated by deer. Less hardy, so-called Italian oregano, *Origanum ×majoricum*, is also called hardy sweet marjoram or knotted marjoram. Its aroma is not as intense as Greek oregano, and it is best used fresh. This confusing common nomenclature is irritating, but one taste or smell tells you the best plant. The leaves can be used fresh or dried; its essential oil is used extensively medicinally for bronchial complaints and in perfumery.

This mat-forming hardy perennial from Greece is slightly hairy, with 1-in. oval leaves and clusters of white flowers in summer. The leaves are evergreen so can be plucked throughout the winter unless blanketed with snow.

HOW TO GROW

Set out young plants after the danger of frost. Select a sunny, well-drained site or grow plants in containers and set them by the kitchen door for easy harvesting. Although Greek oregano tolerates drought well once it is established in the ground, new and potted plants may need extra water. Trim in early spring and after blooming to retain vigor. Unless you can get cuttings from a friend, be sure to buy from a reliable mail-order or local nursery, and sniff the leaves before buying. Seeds are available too, but they do not always produce well-flavored seedlings.

QUICK LOOK

Hardiness
Zones 5–9
Height and spread
1–3 ft. × 1–2 ft.
Deer resistance rating
9–10

DESIGN TIPS

Several kinds of oregano are well worth growing as ornamentals. Golden-leaved cultivars of *Origanum vulgare* are decorative in rock gardens, in containers, and along pathways. 'Aureum' (golden oregano) and 'Aureum Crispum' ('Curly Gold') make dense mats of yellow foliage. White-flowered hardy sweet marjoram (*O.* ×*majoricum*), not to be confused with sweet or knotted oregano (*O. majorana*), is a 2-ft. tall sterile hybrid. Plant it as an edging with other annuals (cleome, flowering tobacco).

Origanum rotundifolium 'Kent Beauty' is an ornamental gem for zones 5 to 8. In summer, hoplike clusters of ¾-in., apple green and rosy pink bracts surround tiny pink flowers that are borne at the tips of wiry, 4- to 5-in. stems. Plant this treasure tumbling over rocks or a sunny wall where drainage is excellent. The mounding stems of evergreen, 12-in. dittany of Crete or hop marjoram (*O. dictamnus*, zones 8 to 10) are clothed with aromatic, fuzzy, rounded, gray-green leaves. In midsummer elongated clusters of fragrant, ½-in., pink flowers nestle among deep pink or purple papery bracts. Bees and butterflies are frequent visitors. This plant is excellent for hanging baskets and rock gardens. Overwinter it indoors with care where winters are cold. In summer through fall, loose whorls of tubular, ½-in., purplish flowers on slender, branching, 1- to 2-ft. flower stems rise above the dark basal foliage of ornamental oregano (*O. laevigatum*, zones 6 to 10). 'Herrenhausen' has maroon buds and pink flowers; 'Hopley's Purple' has purple flowers; 18-in. tall 'Pilgrim' is rosy red. Plant with perennials and shrubs in full sun where drainage is good. All are ideal where water is scarce. Butterflies and bees enjoy their nectar.

The leaves are evergreen so can be plucked throughout the winter unless blanketed with snow.

Prostrate *Origanum vulgare* 'Aureum Crispum' produces yellow, wrinkled leaves.

Rosemary

Rosmarinus officinalis

NO HERB GARDEN is complete without bushes of rosemary, or dew-of-the-sea, but these tender evergreen shrubs are splendid as ornamentals in other parts of the garden, too. Native to sunny, dry coastal regions of the Mediterranean, rosemary tolerates drought, poor stony soil, and salt spray with ease. The essential oils that give the plant its medicinal properties and refreshing piney fragrance are concentrated when rosemary is grown lean and hungry. Herb lovers with sensitive noses maintain that each cultivar has a slightly different smell. It is the strong aroma of the needle leaves that deer dislike.

Rosemary makes dense, rounded or upright bushes of woody stems clothed in aromatic, dusty green, needlelike, 1- to 2-in. leaves that are whitish beneath. Whorls of blue, sometimes white or pink, two-lipped, tubular flowers are carried in the upper leaf axils. Bloom time is usually from winter into spring and early summer.

For centuries, peoples around the globe have used rosemary to treat various ailments and included it in weddings, funerals, and other religious ceremonies. Rosemary is used in countless recipes, particularly in Mediterranean cooking, and rosemary honey is a special delicacy.

HOW TO GROW

In cool winter climates rosemary is fine indoors in either clay or plastic pots; the latter dries out more slowly, and overwatering can be more difficult during short winter days with little air movement. Plant in a free-draining soilless mix, and set in the sunniest window available, ideally at about 65°F. Note that even with all the experienced care in the world, overwintering rosemary indoors is seldom

QUICK LOOK

Hardiness
Zones 7–11
Height and spread
1–7 ft. × 4–5 ft.
Deer resistance rating
9–10

Rosemary (*Rosmarinus officinalis*).

reliable in northern regions. Sometimes the plants just pack up and die.

Harvest rosemary sprigs frequently for cooking and to encourage bushy new growth. Long branches may be stripped of foliage and used as barbeque skewers.

DESIGN TIPS

Numerous rosemary cultivars are available varying in hardiness, size, habit, aroma, and flower color. 'Madeline Hill' (also known as 'Hill Hardy') and 'Arp' are the most hardy; they will survive 0°F and a little below. For general landscape use, upright varieties such as compact 'Blue Spire', stiff 7-ft. tall 'Tuscan Blue', or 5- to 6-ft. tall 'Miss Jessop's Upright' are appropriate. Plant them in mixed borders with drought-tolerant plants such as hummingbird mints, yarrow, and lavender. In herb gardens grow them to line pathways, as hedges, or to accompany pot marigolds, basils, or scented geraniums. 'Blue Spire' makes a great specimen in a tub or barrel by the kitchen door in zone 9 or warmer. Rosemary does well in seaside gardens and is especially attractive sculpted by the wind. It is a natural candidate for bee and butterfly gardens, as well as fragrance gardens. Allow low-growing varieties such as 'Irene' and 'Prostrata' to tumble over rocks and walls. They are suitable also for hanging baskets and bonsai. Clipped topiary cones and standards are popular gifts for passionate cooks.

Herb lovers with sensitive noses maintain that each cultivar has a slightly different smell.

Sage

Salvia officinalis

SAGE IS an all-time favorite, as impressive as an ornamental as it is for culinary use. Its handsome, oval, gray-green, pungently aromatic, 3-in. leaves, and spikes of purple-blue summer flowers, equip it for a place in many areas besides the herb garden. The foliage is a good foil for flowers and shrubs alike, and the stems are useful for flower arrangements with gray-leaved yarrow, pinks, and foxgloves, among others. Sage has a very strong odor of camphor, which comes from the essential oils mostly in the leaves. Growing it lean and dry will concentrate the essential oils. Deer dislike the aroma, and sage is also reported to control carrot flies and other pests in vegetable gardens. Meanwhile, butterflies, bees (sage honey is good), and other pollinators are attracted to it in wildlife gardens.

Sage has been used medicinally since Roman times and was frequently grown in medieval monastery gardens. The leaves are used to make tea and are a favorite flavoring for pork, goose, and turkey stuffing. The edible flowers adorn salads and savory dishes. Pale green Sage Derby cheese is a special treat. Sage oil is used commercially in toothpastes and cosmetics.

HOW TO GROW

Evergreen, aromatic sage grows wild in sunny Mediterranean regions where the soil is alkaline, dry, and poor. Try to simulate these conditions for best results. Good drainage is essential, and fertilizer is seldom required. To encourage young new growth, prune woody stems in late spring. Plants need to be replaced after several years. Cuttings of soft young growth are easy to root, or stems can be layered.

QUICK LOOK

Hardiness
Zones 4–8
Height and spread
1–3 ft. × 2–3 ft.
Deer resistance rating
9–10

DESIGN TIPS

There is more to sage than plain gray-green. Among the cultivars available, a few stand out. 'Berggarten' has larger, rounded gray leaves, useful for stuffing with peanut butter, pâté, or cream cheese, or deep-fried for a crunchy nibble. Golden variegated sage, 'Icterina', has very attractive greenish leaves irregularly edged with subtle gold. It seldom tops 18 in. tall and is an interesting companion for signet marigolds (*Tagetes tenuifolia*), threadleaf coreopsis (*Coreopsis verticillata*), and creeping zinnia (*Sanvitalia procumbens*) in rock gardens. Some gardeners seem to have a love-hate relationship with 'Tricolor'. Its gray-green foliage is variegated with pink, cream, and purple, especially when young. It is not as hardy or as large as other cultivars but is suitable for rock gardens or on top of low walls. It is also a lively partner for parsley, basil, rosemary, and other plain green herbs. Try using 'Tricolor' as a topper for a terra-cotta strawberry pot filled with herbs. Purple-leaved plants are popular, and 'Purpurascens' sage is no exception. Try it as a skirt around golden Hinoki false cypress (*Chamaecyparis obtusa* 'Nana Gracilis') or beside 'Hidcote' lavender (*Lavandula angustifolia* 'Hidcote'). An underplanting of trailing golden creeping Jenny (*Lysimachia nummularia* 'Aurea') sets it off well. Late-blooming, tender, red-flowered pineapple sage (*Salvia elegans*) has pea green leaves with a strong pineapple scent—excellent in fruit salad. All sages make good container subjects alone or in combination with other sun lovers.

Butterflies, bees (sage honey is good), and other pollinators are attracted to it in wildlife gardens.

Sage (*Salvia officinalis*).

Thyme

Thymus vulgaris

THOUGH SOMETIMES called English thyme, this evergreen, bushy little shrub is native to southern Europe and Asia, growing in bright sun in poor, often limey soil. The aromatic, ¼- to ½-in., gray-green leaves are used fresh or dried in a multitude of dishes. In late spring and summer, short spikes of tiny, tubular, purple, pink, or white flowers appear that attract plenty of bees and butterflies.

Thyme has been valued through the centuries by numerous cultures for its medicinal and flavoring properties and was even an embalming herb for the Egyptians. An essential herb in Herbes de Provence, it imparts intense flavor to any meat or vegetable dish. Some even put it in ice cream, and thyme honey is delicious. The intense aroma keeps deer at bay.

HOW TO GROW

Thyme is easy to start from seed but more often is bought as young plants from garden centers. Plant in full sun, and grow it lean and dry for the most pungent essential oils to develop. Good drainage is essential; add lime chips or an oyster shell mulch to sweeten acid soil. Thymes are not very successful in hot and humid climates, as the plants tend to "melt down" in the heat, but keeping them cut back helps to alleviate this problem. The essential oils reach their peak just before bloom time, so harvest leaves when flowers are budding. Keeping the mounds of foliage cut back encourages young growth, but inevitably plants become woody, decline, and need replacement after a few years. Layer or take summer cuttings of special selections.

QUICK LOOK

Hardiness
Zones 4–9
Height and spread
6–12 in. × 12–16 in.
Deer resistance rating
9–10

The foliage of *Thymus vulgaris* 'Silver Posie' is rimmed with silver.

In late spring and summer, short spikes of tiny, tubular, purple, pink, or white flowers appear that attract plenty of bees and butterflies.

DESIGN TIPS

Selections of *Thymus vulgaris* abound, some with different aromas. 'Orange Balsam' is one of the more exotic, with a pronounced citrus fragrance that brightens many meat and fish dishes. Popular 'Silver Posie' and 'Argenteus' have silver-rimmed leaves. Other species of thyme are worth growing. Less than 1 in. tall, creeping thyme (*T. serpyllum*), also known as mother-of-thyme or wild thyme, is perfect for growing beside paths, between pavers and rocks, and as a flat groundcover, perhaps under lavender or sages. It tolerates light foot traffic and emits a spicy scent when bruised. 'Elfin' is a little taller. Woolly thyme (*T. pseudolanuginosus*) also grows close to the ground and is used between stepping stones; in dry rock gardens, partner it with pinks (*Dianthus*) and creeping oreganos (*Origanum*). The carpet of gray, woolly leaves is soft underfoot. 'Minor' is an adorable miniature. A fall-blooming hybrid, lemon thyme (*T. ×citriodorus*) has an upright, bushy habit and refreshing lemony fragrance that makes it popular in fish dishes. Selections include golden lemon thyme ('Aureus') with bright gold-speckled leaves, and 'Argenteus' and 'Hi-Ho Silver', both edged with silvery white.

Any of the upright growers are suitable as edging plants in herb or vegetable gardens, can tumble between boulders in rock gardens, or can decorate the front of flower borders. Since they tolerate drought well, use this attribute on banks, berms, or otherwise neglected places where water is not available. They also take shearing well and are attractive as low hedges in herb gardens and mazes.

Grasses

The fat, stiff bottlebrush flowers of black fountain grass (*Pennisetum alopecuroides* 'Moudry', bottom right) provide contrast in this ornamental grass garden.

Fountain grass

Pennisetum alopecuroides

FOUNTAIN GRASS or swamp foxtail grass produces bristly cylindrical spikes of flowers that catch the eye from early summer through fall. It is almost irresistible to touch and is a favorite of youngsters. Deer avoid the sharp leaf edges; maybe the feathery flower spikes tickle, too. This warm-season clumping grass is native to temperate and tropical regions of the world; in cold areas the related tropical species showy fountain grass (*Pennisetum setaceum*) and feathertop (*P. villosum*) are grown as annuals.

With its abundant, bright green, ¼- to ½-in. wide leaves and strongly rounded habit, fountain grass is easy to integrate into most sunny residential gardens. As the temperature drops in fall, the foliage turns yellow and brown, bleaching out to cream as the season progresses. Bottle-brush-like flower spikes are borne on arching stems above the mass of foliage. These may reach 10 in. long and up to 3 in. wide in cream, silvery pink, pinkish brown, tan, or even black depending upon the selection.

HOW TO GROW

Set out young plants in spring 3 to 4 ft. apart in full sun. They tolerate most soils including those in seaside gardens. Provide sufficient soil moisture; fountain grass is drought tolerant when established. Cut down the leaves in early spring. In fall the flower spikes begin to shatter; remove the spikes to prevent self-seeding.

DESIGN TIPS

Just a single plant makes a statement in the landscape or in a container, but fountain grass can also be a dramatic foil for woody bluebeards (*Caryopteris ×clandonensis*), Thunberg bush clover (*Lespedeza thunbergii*), and Russian

QUICK LOOK

Hardiness
Zones 5–9
Height and spread
2–5 ft. × 2–4 ft.
Deer resistance rating
9–10

'Hameln' fountain grass (*Pennisetum alopecuroides* 'Hameln').

It is almost irresistible to touch and is a favorite of youngsters.

sage (*Perovskia*). Try any of these, especially set off by 'Moudry', the black fountain grass. Hummingbird mints (*Agastache*), purple coneflowers (*Echinacea*), and other perennials are fine companions for fountain grass in beds and borders. Annual partners might include spider flower (*Cleome*) and flowering tobacco (*Nicotiana*), for example. Perfectly in scale in rock gardens, the informal habit and movement provided by 18-in. tall 'Hameln' and 9- to 12-in. tall 'Little Bunny' (both zones 6 to 9) are a joy. They are valuable companions with low shrubs, including boxwood (*Buxus*) and dwarf cultivars of Japanese holly. The dramatic but late-appearing inflorescences of 'Moudry' and similar 'National Arboretum' age to purple-black. They do extremely well in mild Southern California but may not mature before frost in northern regions. Be careful of excessive self-seeding. Heat-tolerant, evergreen *Pennisetum* 'Fairy Tails' (zones 5 to 9) is a welcome sterile hybrid, especially in Southern California. Its pink flowers rise well above the mass of foliage on strong stems, and turn tan with age.

Another species, oriental fountain grass (*Pennisetum orientale*, zones 7 to 9), is notable for its spring-to-frost bloom time and slender pink plumes. The inflorescences of 3-ft. tall 'Karley Rose' mature to dusky purple, while 'Tall Tails' (5 to 6 ft. tall) has elegant, drooping flower stems and good orange fall color. It is spectacular with large yarrows and monkshoods. Purple fountain grass (*P. setaceum* 'Rubrum', zones 9 to 10) may be the most popular for mixed summer containers, where it adds height and grace. Its strong, gently arching habit and purple foliage enliven more ho-hum annuals such as wax begonias. For a change, try it with pink or lavender peony poppies, spider flower (*Cleome*), or annual larkspur (*Consolida ajacis*).

Hakone grass

Hakonechloa macra

THIS MOST beautiful grass from the mountains of Japan has become popular in the United States and Canada. Contrary to many reports, Hakone grass (also known as Japanese forest grass) tolerates winters in zone 6, and possibly zone 5, especially where there is snow cover. As with most ornamental grasses, the sharp leaf edges deter deer.

Hakone grass is deciduous, with bright green, 4- to 6-in. long, bamboolike leaves. These are carried on slender, weeping stems so that the foliage overlaps to form flowing layers. Delicate sprays of flower spikelets appear in late summer, adding to the elegance of this grass. By early fall the leaves begin to change color, turning a rosy pink and then bronze in part sun or tan in light shade (although Hakone grass will grow in deeper shade, leaf color will be poor). The foliage holds on through the winter and is pretty dusted with snow.

HOW TO GROW

Put out young plants about 15 in. apart in spring. Select a partly shaded spot where the soil drains well but retains summer moisture. The addition of compost at planting time is beneficial. If the soil tends to be dry, add a summer mulch of compost around the plants to keep them moist. Division is seldom necessary except to increase stock in spring or fall.

DESIGN TIPS

Hakone grass is valuable as a groundcover, although it spreads slowly and does not bulk up as rapidly as some. It is also useful to soften the edges of paths and walkways, and is appropriate grouped in shaded meadow plantings.

QUICK LOOK

Hardiness
Zones 6–9
Height and spread
12 in. × 12 in.
Deer resistance rating
9–10

Although the all-green species is appealing, some really nice variegated selections are on the market, all of which give at least three seasons of interest (but tend to be less vigorous). 'Aureola', the most widely grown, has bright yellow leaves striped with green. A well-grown plant in dappled shade is stunningly beautiful, but too much sun bleaches it out and too much shade causes the color to fade. Fall color is pinkish tan. Use this cultivar to lighten up shaded corners; in the ground with other shade lovers such as astilbes, barrenworts, and ferns; or alone cascading over a rock or container. The striped green, yellow, and cream foliage of 'Albo-aurea' is less vibrant than 'Aureola'. Slow-spreading 'Naomi' is similar but with much stronger purple autumn color. Let it drape over rocks and walls. Easy-care, all-green 'Beni-kaze' (meaning "red wind") turns red in fall; orange and red foliage distinguish 'Nicolas' in cool fall weather. White-striped 'Albo-striata' has broad green leaves decorated with narrow and wider white stripes. It grows faster than some cultivars and is particularly attractive beside ponds or streams. 'All Gold', vigorous and quick to bulk up, is more upright but shorter; its completely golden leaves have the same cascading habit. Try this on the edge of woods in dramatic contrast to black-leaved branched bugbane (*Actaea ramosa* 'Brunette') and perhaps black-stemmed maidenhair fern (*Adiantum*). Solo in a decorative container, it is a knock out.

Delicate sprays of flower spikelets appear in late summer, adding to the elegance of this grass.

'Aureola' Hakone grass (*Hakonechloa macra* 'Aureola').

201

Japanese sweet flag

Acorus gramineus

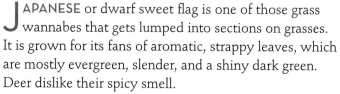

JAPANESE or dwarf sweet flag is one of those grass wannabes that gets lumped into sections on grasses. It is grown for its fans of aromatic, strappy leaves, which are mostly evergreen, slender, and a shiny dark green. Deer dislike their spicy smell.

Native to Japan and eastern Asia, Japanese sweet flag is found growing in shallow standing water or wet places beside ponds, lakes, and streams. Its aroid flowers appear in summer but usually only if the plants are growing in water. Slowly spreading rhizomes gradually grow into wide clumps, producing compact fans of foliage that tolerate foot traffic. Japanese sweet flag does well along damp pathways and emits a pleasing cinnamon fragrance when bruised. Use some of the smaller cultivars, such as 5-in. tall 'Pusillus', golden 'Pusillus Minimus Aureus', or white-variegated, 6-in. tall 'Masamune', to plant between stepping stones.

HOW TO GROW

This plant prefers wet or boggy soils but will do fine in meadows and gardens as long as soil remains moist. In the South and West, where sun is intense, supply some shade to protect it from browning and burning. Select plants from the garden center in spring and plant them about 6 to 12 in. apart in wet soil. Prepare the soil by adding plenty of organic matter to help retain moisture. An organic mulch in summer is beneficial. In perennial and shrub borders Japanese sweet flag will need extra irrigation for the best-looking foliage. Plant it with moisture-loving astilbes, turtleheads, and Japanese iris. To build stock, divide the rhizomes in spring.

QUICK LOOK

Hardiness
Zones 6–10
Height and spread
8–12 in. × 12 in.
Deer resistance rating
9–10

Golden variegated sweet flag
(*Acorus gramineus* 'Ogon').

Japanese sweet flag does well along damp pathways and emits a pleasing cinnamon fragrance when bruised.

DESIGN TIPS

Golden variegated sweet flag (*Acorus gramineus* 'Ogon') is possibly the most popular cultivar. Its intense yellow, 10-in. leaves arch at the tips and lighten up any spot where it is planted. It does well in large tubs or water gardens and beside ponds and lakes. Partner it with annual monkey flower (*Mimulus guttatus*) and Japanese iris, underplanted with pennyroyal (*Mentha pulegium*). Chameleon flower (*Houttuynia cordata* 'Chameleon') is another beautiful companion, with pale green, cream, and pink foliage, but be sure to grow it where the roots are confined, as it invades rapidly. Variegated Japanese sweet flag (*A. gramineus* 'Variegatus') is an old variety with 6- to 12-in. long, cream-and-green-striped leaves. It is attractive massed as a groundcover in damp soil at the front of partly shaded flower borders and foundation plantings. When it is planted on slippery banks, the rhizomes help to control erosion.

Closely related sweet flag (*Acorus calamus*), or calamus, is also desirable for wet places. Numerous cultures have used it historically as an anointing oil and in medicine, and it was a fragrant strewing herb in medieval times. The dried root is still used in some homeopathic preparations and as a fixative in perfumes. Some also use it as a love potion or aphrodisiac, but calamus oil is toxic. 'Variegatus' is planted for its 3-ft. long, longitudinally striped, green and white leaves. Grow a clump in a large container in a shallow pool. Scouring rush (*Equisetum hyemale*), also grown in a container at pool bottom, is a striking companion, but do not plant it at water's edge since it is very invasive and difficult to remove. *Cyperus papyrus* 'King Tut' would complete the picture.

Morrow's sedge

Carex morrowii

BOTANIST JAMES MORROW discovered Morrow's sedge, also called Japanese sedge, in the low mountains of Japan during the famous Perry expedition to China and Japan in the mid-19th century. It is an evergreen, grasslike perennial valued as a weed-controlling groundcover or for the front of shaded borders. Its saw-toothed leaves may be what causes deer to pass it by, although deer avoid most species of sedge. Many cultivars of this and other sedges are on the market. The cultivars of *Carex morrowii* are grown more often than the species itself.

The 1-in. wide, stiff, flattened leaves of Morrow's sedge grow into dense tufts. In spring, clusters of green and brown flower spikelets appear. The male spikelets are carried at the tips of the triangular flowering stems; two or three females emerge further down the stem.

HOW TO GROW

Set out plants in spring, about 12 in. apart in soil rich in organic matter. You can also plant them more closely as a groundcover, but their attractive habit will be lost. These rhizomatous plants spread and thrive in moist soil in lightly shaded places. They do well in heavy shade too, but not in full sun. When well established, Morrow's sedge tolerates drought conditions. If it is planted in dry shade, keep it well watered until it is settled. Maintenance is low. A summer mulch of organic material such as compost or decomposed wood chips helps to retain soil moisture. Cut back the old foliage in spring to allow the new leaves to develop. Divide the clumps in spring every few years.

QUICK LOOK

Hardiness
Zones 5–9
Height and spread
12–18 in. × 12 in.
Deer resistance rating
9–10

DESIGN TIPS

Some of the showiest cultivars include 1-ft. tall 'Gold-band', a slightly upright grower with green leaves rimmed with gold. 'Aureo-variegata' is similar but a little taller with stiffer leaves. Either of these is attractive with 'Brazen Hussy' lesser celandine (*Ranunculus ficaria* 'Brazen Hussy') or marsh marigolds (*Caltha palustris*) if there is enough light. Yellow double meadow buttercup (*Ranunculus acris* 'Flore Pleno') is another successful, though spreading, companion. 'Variegata' may be the most widely grown form in containers, along woodland paths, and as a groundcover under trees. It makes a clumping fountain of dark green leaves edged with silvery white. 'Ice Dance' is a dead ringer for 'Variegata' but spreads slowly. Its white-edged, ½-in. wide, arching leaves mimic a variegated lilyturf (*Liriope*), which deer browse freely. 'Silk Tassel' has hairy, silver leaves edged in green. The wispy foliage is as fine as silk, on clumps up to 2 ft. across. Use it to brighten shady, damp spots in the garden, perhaps with mace sedge (*Carex grayi*) and yellow flag iris (*Iris pseudacorus*). At the Scott Arboretum of Swarthmore College, 'Silk Tassel' is a favorite for winter containers. It highlights mixed pots with many deer-resistant plants, including tassel fern (*Polystichum polyblepharum*), Japanese umbrella pine (*Sciadopitys verticillata*), and barrenwort. Fine-textured 'Silver Sceptre' makes silvery tousled clumps of white-margined, ¼-in. wide leaves. Group this Japanese introduction among ferns in woodland gardens, or grow it in a "drop container" to brighten a dense patch of pachysandra or other dull groundcover.

The white-edged, ½-in. wide, arching leaves of 'Ice Dance' mimic a variegated lilyturf (*Liriope*), which deer browse freely.

Morrow's sedge (*Carex morrowii*).

Switch grass

Panicum virgatum

THIS CLUMPING GRASS is native across the United States and Canada, south to Florida and west to the Rockies. It was a major species of the tallgrass prairie and is now making news as a possible source for biofuels. Colorful selections have made switch grass a favorite ornamental too, especially since deer find the sharp-edged leaves unpalatable (as with most ornamental grasses). Switch grass requires little care, has amazing fall color, and provides a strong vertical accent in the garden. Its autumn colors and winter presence make it effective as a temporary hedge or barrier.

Warm-season switch grass produces clouds of tiny flower spikelets in mid- to late summer. These give an ethereal effect, contrasting well with dark evergreens. Site where the plants are backlit to appreciate them spangled with dew or after a shower. The ¼- to ½-in. wide leaves are a deep grayish green, but some cultivars are blue or have maroon or reddish highlights all season; several are spectacular in fall.

HOW TO GROW

Full sun and moist soil are ideal, but switch grass tolerates a wide range of soils, growing even in boggy areas and drier places. The stiff flower stems grow in a tight column in full sun but relax more in shade. Set young plants out 3 to 4 ft. apart in spring or fall. Keep new plantings moist, and divide crowded plants every three to four years. The tan, dry flower stems remain through the winter unless smothered by heavy snow; cut down in early spring to 12 to 18 in.

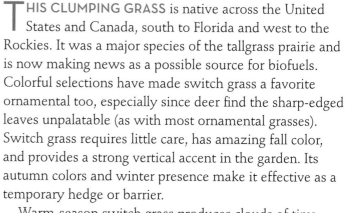

QUICK LOOK

Hardiness
Zones 5–9
Height and spread
3–4 ft. × 2–2½ ft.
Deer resistance rating
9–10

Switch grass (*Panicum virgatum*) grows alongside a path.

Switch grass requires little care, has amazing fall color, and provides a strong vertical accent in the garden.

DESIGN TIPS

Among the bluest of the blue-leaved selections, 3- to 7-ft. tall 'Dallas Blues' is spectacular. Somewhat hardier than the species, it has reddish mauve or plum flower heads, beautiful against Japanese andromeda (*Pieris japonica*). Check out the mass planting on Chicago Botanic Garden's Evening Island, where the switch grass provides a food source and haven for birds and other wildlife. 'Heavy Metal' is another good blue, 3½ ft. tall with deep burgundy flowers rising another 15 in. above. Try it alongside giant coneflower (*Rudbeckia maxima*). Both 6- to 8-ft. tall 'Cloud Nine' and broad-leaved, 4- to 6-ft. tall 'Northwind' are also reliable blue-leaved selections. All have golden fall color. Partner any of these with tall verbena (*Verbena bonariensis*), azure monkshood (*Aconitum carmichaelii*), or yellow and orange selections of purple coneflower (*Echinacea*). 'Shenandoah' is a very hardy 2- to 3-ft. tall selection of 4-ft. tall 'Haense Herms', with better red and burgundy coloration.

Switch grass works well in many locations, but beware of seeding about. Plant three or five together in meadows, wildflower gardens, and native plant gardens. Butterfly weed (*Asclepias tuberosa*), purple coneflower, goldenrod (*Solidago*), and Joe-Pye weed (*Eupatorium purpureum*) are all appropriate companions (in addition to asters, which some report as deer food in their area). Groupings of switch grass also look dramatic against bold-foliaged castor bean (*Ricinus*), and *Rosa rugosa* makes an attractive companion in coastal gardens. Use the flower and seed sprays as cut flowers both fresh and dried.

Resources for Mail-Order Plants

This list represents just a brief selection of mail-order sources. Check local garden centers and nurseries for high-quality plants before sending off for the same plant by mail. Plants received through the mail will be smaller to save shipping costs and will have endured the stress of transit. Many local sources have great selections.

Beaver Creek Greenhouses .... www.rockgardenplants.com
Bluestone Perennials .... www.bluestoneperennials.com
Brent and Becky's Bulbs .... www.brentandbeckybulbs.com
Deer-Resistant Landscape Nursery .... www.deerxlandscape.com
Fairweather Gardens .... www.fairweathergardens.com
Fieldstone Gardens .... www.fieldstonegardens.com
Fraser's Thimble Farms .... www.thimblefarms.com
High Country Gardens .... www.highcountrygardens.com
John Scheepers .... www.johnscheepers.com
Joy Creek Nursery .... www.joycreek.com
Klehm's Song Sparrow Perennial Farm .... www.songsparrow.com
Kurt Bluemel .... www.kurtbluemel.com
McClure and Zimmerman .... www.mzbulb.com
Niche Gardens .... www.nichegardens.com
Plant Delights Nursery .... www.plantdelights.com
Prairie Nursery .... www.prairienursery.com
Richters Herbs .... www.richters.com
Select Seeds .... www.selectseeds.com
Van Bourgondien .... www.dutchbulbs.com
Veseys .... www.veseys.com
Wayside Gardens .... www.waysidegardens.com
Well-Sweep Herb Farm .... www.wellsweep.com
White Flower Farm .... www.whiteflowerfarm.com

Glossary

ANNUAL: A plant (floss flower, for example) that germinates from seed, produces flowers and fruit, and dies all within a single season

AROID: Having flowers like an arum or calla lily

BARE-ROOT: Sold from the ground without a pot or soil around the roots

BERM: A mound or wall of soil built to create different levels in a garden

BIENNIAL: A plant (forget-me-not, for example) that completes its life cycle in two years

COMPOST: Vegetative materials such as weeds, plant clippings, household vegetable peelings, and tea and coffee grounds that have decayed and broken down into black, crumbly soil

CONDITION: To strip flower stems of leaves after cutting and place overnight in cool water to harden the stems and engorge the flowers with water prior to arranging

CONTAINERIZED: Grown and sold in containers or pots rather than bare-root or in six-packs

CROSIER: Unfurling fern fronds

CROWN: The part of a plant where the stems and roots meet

CULTIVAR: A cultivated variety that has been developed from and is different from a species. Mostly propagated vegetatively, not by seed

DAPPLED SHADE: Shade found under deciduous trees where sun comes through the foliage. See also *light shade*

DEADHEAD: To remove spent flowers, both for neatness and to encourage a second crop of bloom

DROP CONTAINER: A container that is planted and temporarily dropped complete into a garden bed or border to provide extra interest or color

DRY SHADE: Shade found beneath shallow-rooted deciduous or evergreen trees where root competition for water is strong, or under the eaves of buildings or overhangs that do not receive rain

EXOTIC: Introduced from another country or continent

FROND: Leaf of a fern

FULL SHADE: Shade in which direct sun never shines

FULL SUN: Sun for six or more hours per day

GENUS, GENERA: A group of plants having similar floral characteristics, such as *Dicentra*. The category of plant classification ranking between family and species

HARDINESS ZONE: The United States Department of Agriculture system used to determine if a particular plant will survive the winter in your area. For example, a plant hardy to zone 5 is expected to survive winter temperatures of −10°F to −20°F

HERBACEOUS: Having fleshy, not woody, aboveground stems and leaves. An herbaceous perennial dies back to the ground in winter and produces new growth from a crown or rootstock

INDUSIUM, INDUSIA: Kidney-shaped structure covering fern spores

INFLORESCENCE: A cluster of flowers on a stem

LAYER: To propagate a plant (usually woody) by pegging down a low side stem into the soil and partially covering it to encourage rooting, later severing the rooted plant

LIGHT SHADE: Shade usually found under small-foliaged deciduous trees (birch, for example) or where bright light is reflected from buildings. See also *dappled shade*

LIMB UP: To remove lower limbs and over-hanging branches to allow light and air to penetrate, or to remove the browse line to prevent damage by deer

MIDRIB: Main vein of a leaf or frond

NATIVE: Growing naturally in a particular region, historically not introduced from another area

ORGANIC MATTER: Plant and animal residue, including leaves, trimmings, and manure in various stages of decomposition

ORNAMENTAL: Cultivated for decorative flowers or foliage rather than for food

PANICLE: An unbranched inflorescence bearing flowers on branched stems

PART SHADE: Shade created by buildings or dense trees for part of the day, often in early morning or late afternoon

PART SUN: Direct sun for part of the day but less than six hours

PERENNIAL: A plant (peony, for example) that lives for more than two years and blooms annually

PINNA, PINNAE: Leaflet of a fern frond

PROPAGATE: To create new plants

RACEME: A long unbranched inflorescence with stemmed flowers

RACHIS: The main vein of a fern frond

RHIZOME: A horizontal underground stem often swollen with stored food. Rhizomes may be branched or not and are divided for propagation

ROOTSTOCK: An underground stem with roots and buds for the following year's growth

SCAT: Droppings

SELECTION: A superior plant that has been chosen from seed trials over several generations

SOFT BUD: A flower bud that is still tight but squishy to the touch, not hard

SPECIES: The basic unit of plant classification, representing a group of closely related plants, such as *Dicentra eximia*

SPIKE: An unbranched inflorescence with flowers attached directly to the stem

SPIKELET: A small spike, especially in grasses

STIPE: The stem of a fern frond

SUBSPECIES: The category of plant classification one step down from species

THRILLER: A bold, usually upright plant used as a focal point in containers

TILTH: A fine, crumbly soil texture

VARIETY: May refer to any plant that is different from and ranked below a species. Often used interchangeably with the term *cultivar*, though this is incorrect. Especially used with vegetables

VEGETATIVE PROPAGATION: To make new plants by division, cuttings, layering, or other vegetative means, not by seed

VELVET: The soft covering that nurtures the antlers of bucks

WELL-DRAINED: Draining freely, without puddling after a few minutes

WOODY: Having stems that are hard and that do not die back in winter due to the presence of lignin

XERIC GARDEN: A garden in which water is sparse and plants must tolerate dry conditions well

ZONE: See *hardiness zone*

Further Reading

Adler, Bill, Jr. 1999. *Outwitting Deer*. Lyons Press, New York.

Armitage, Allan M. 1998. *Herbaceous Perennial Plants*. 2nd edition. Stipes, Champaign, IL.

Armitage, Allan M. 2004. *Armitage's Garden Annuals*. Timber Press, Portland, OR.

Barash, Cathy Wilkinson. 1997. *Edible Flowers*. Fulcrum, Golden, CO.

Brickell, Christopher, and H. Marc Cathey, eds. 2004. *The American Horticultural Society A–Z Encyclopedia of Garden Plants*. DK Publishing, New York.

Buchanan, Rita, ed. 1995. *Taylor's Guide to Herbs*. Houghton Mifflin, Boston.

Clausen, Ruth Rogers, and Nicolas H. Ekstrom. 1989. *Perennials for American Gardens*. Random House, New York.

Darke, Rick. 2007. *The Encyclopedia of Grasses for Livable Landscapes*. Timber Press, Portland, OR.

Dirr, Michael. 1997. *Dirr's Hardy Trees and Shrubs*. Timber Press, Portland, OR.

Dirr, Michael. 1998. *Manual of Woody Landscape Plants*. Stipes, Champaign, IL.

Disabato-Aust, Tracy. 2006. *The Well-Tended Perennial Garden*. Expanded edition. Timber Press, Portland, OR.

Drzewucki, Vincent, Jr. 1998. *Gardening in Deer Country*. Brick Tower Press, New York.

Glassberg, Jeffrey. 2002. *Butterflies of North America*. Friedman/Fairfax, New York.

Greenlee, John. 2009. *The American Meadow Garden*. Timber Press, Portland, OR.

Harper, Pamela J. 2000. *Time-Tested Plants*. Timber Press, Portland, OR.

Heath, Brent, and Becky Heath. 2001. *Daffodils for North American Gardens*. Bright Sky Press, Albany, TX.

Hoffman, M. H. A. 2005. *List of Plant Names of Perennials*. 5th fully revised edition. Applied Plant Research, Netherlands.

Hoffman, M. H. A. 2005. *List of Plant Names of Woody Plants*. 7th fully revised edition. Applied Plant Research, Netherlands.

Jescavage-Bernard, Karen. 1991. *Gardening in Deer Country*. K. Jescavage-Bernard.

Mickel, John. 2003. *Ferns for American Gardens*. Macmillan, New York.

Mineo, Baldassare. 1999. *Rock Garden Plants*. Timber Press, Portland, OR.

Robinson, William. 1895. *The Wild Garden*. Expanded edition. Timber Press, Portland, OR, 2009.

Saville, Carol. 1997. *Exotic Herbs*. Henry Holt, New York.

Singer, Carolyn. 2006. *Deer in My Garden*. 2 vols. Garden Wisdom Press, Grass Valley, CA.

Summers, Carolyn. 2010. *Designing Gardens with Flora of the American East*. Rutgers University Press, New Brunswick, NJ.

Tenenbaum, Frances. 1997. *Taylor's Dictionary for Gardeners*. Houghton Mifflin, Boston.

Tenenbaum, Frances, ed. 2003. *Taylor's Garden Guides: Encyclopedia of Garden Plants*. Houghton Mifflin, Boston.

Index

About the Author

© Dorian Winslow

Ruth Rogers Clausen's *Perennials for American Gardens* (Random House, 1989, with coauthor Nicolas H. Ekstrom) received the Quill and Trowel Award for 1990 from the Garden Writers Association. She has also written for the American Garden Guides series: *Perennial Gardening* with The New York Botanical Garden, *Annual Gardening* with Missouri Botanical Garden, and *Trees* with Chicago Botanic Garden. Her *Dreamscaping* was published by Hearst Books. Ruth has contributed articles to several of the Brooklyn Botanic Garden's Handbooks and Reader's Digest Books. The former horticulture editor for *Country Living Gardener* magazine, Ruth contributes articles to several magazines including *Country Gardens, Organic Gardening, Horticulture,* and *Fine Gardening.* She gardens in Westchester County, New York, where deer abound.

About the Photographer

Linda Detrick

Alan L. Detrick is a professional photographer whose images of nature and gardens appear in media worldwide. He has lectured and conducted photography workshops at Maine Media Workshops, the New York Botanical Garden, and Chanticleer Gardens, as well as for the American Horticultural Society, the Garden Club of America, and the Garden Writers Association, where he was elected into the Hall of Fame in 2010. He is the author and photographer for *Macro Photography for Gardeners and Nature Lovers.*